The Schizophrenic Church

The Schizophrenic Church

Conflict Over Community Organization

by Robert Lee and Russell Galloway
with assistance of William Eichorn

The Westminister Press · Philadelphia

A project by the Institute of Ethics and Society, San
Francisco Theological Seminary, commissioned by the
Division of Lay Education and the Office of Church and
Society of the Board of Christian Education, The United
Presbyterian Church U.S.A.

STANDARD BOOK NO. 664-24841-1

LIBRARY OF CONGRESS CATALOG CARD NO. 69-12490

PUBLISHED BY THE WESTMINSTER PRESS ®
PHILADELPHIA, PENNSYLVANIA

PRINTED IN THE UNITED STATES OF AMERICA

Preface

Ever since the publication of *Religion and Social Conflict*, based on lectures sponsored by the Institute of Ethics and Society at San Francisco Theological Seminary, the Institute has had a continuing interest in the subject of conflict. When the "Alinsky controversy" erupted in the Bay Area during the spring of 1966, it presented an unusual opportunity to explore this subject more intensively. Here was a dramatic instance of conflict in the church over its participation in a prominent strategy of social change.

Happily our interest dovetailed with the concerns of the Board of Christian Education's Project CLEAR, a social education emphasis of the Division of Lay Education and the Office of Church and Society of The United Presbyterian Church U.S.A. "CLEAR" stands for Communication, Liaison, Experimentation, and Action Research concerning the church's ministry and mission in conflict. Project CLEAR's basic purpose is "to explore resources and strategies for interpreting, participating in, dealing with, and sometimes initiating conflict in church and community in order that conflict may be civilizing and reconciling rather than destructive." Thus under the staff direction of Project CLEAR's director, Dieter T. Hessel, the Board of Christian Education authorized a modest grant to support a study focusing on the dynamics of presby-

tery and parish decision-making in response to church involvement in community organization.

Even though the case study approach deals with one episode in a particular locale, THE SCHIZOPHRENIC CHURCH is no
isolated case in a corner of the nation pertaining solely to a
single denomination. Rather, we have here a microcosm of
church-community conflict. Our findings will shed light on
the understanding of churches in conflict everywhere. Although the study's setting is the San Francisco Bay Area, our
findings have a wider relevance and may easily be transposed
beyond the Bay Area or the San Francisco Presbytery. In this
connection we call the reader's attention to Part Three of this
volume, which pinpoints the necessity of conflict management and suggests various strategies for coping with conflict.

Our purpose in this study is threefold and corresponds to
the three-part division of the volume.

First, we seek to chronicle the events of an intense episode
of church conflict, lest it lapse into oblivion as a fuzzy memory.
This documentation of contemporary history is a task more
complex and difficult than would appear at first blush. One
must have some psychological distance, some sense of detach-
ment, simply to sort out the available facts of a controversy
that is so emotion-laden and that evokes such polarized responses. Although we have sought to be faithful in unraveling
the complexity and to be sensitive to the variety of special
claims, it is predictable that none of the parties to the controversy will concur wholeheartedly with our analysis. Indeed,
some will feel hurt, slighted, or offended. Our hope remains,
however, that this volume will not serve to ignite another
round of debate; rather, our hope is to bring not only the
parties involved but also the church at large to a new level
of self-understanding.

Second, we seek to examine and interpret the impact of the
dispute at the local congregational level. Originally six parishes were chosen for depth study to discern the dynamics set
loose by the controversy. Due to space limitations, however,

four of these case studies are presented here to illustrate the diverse spectrum of responses. Although the names of the local churches and personalities are disguised, the events and issues recounted are real. There is no need to get "hung up" on personalities, either for praise or blame, for our task is to clarify and understand the human situation—not to praise or to bury God or Caesar. Readers will surely be tempted to identify with one or another congregation and perhaps to see their own self-image reflected therein. They are encouraged to figure out how they might have responded to the situation.

Third, we seek to gain a better understanding of the nature of conflict and what it portends for the future of church and society. In the intermediate future, few topics will be more crucial for the churches in America. Thus the final portion of the volume comes to grips with a revised understanding of church conflict and points the way to a pluralistic conception of the church which will embrace both sides of its split personality.

A brief word about methodology is in order. Three steps were followed. The first entailed a rather extensive search and survey of the literature on community conflict and related studies. This material was collected and annotated in the form of research notes for further study. Materials from this process are now on file with the Project CLEAR office.

Our second step was the selection of a panel of twenty-five informants who were knowledgeable about the incident and deeply involved in it at the presbytery level. This method of drawing information from so-called "reputational elites" (people that other people think are in the know) meant that our data had to be collated and sifted out and frequently rechecked. Average length of interviews with our panel of informants was two hours. Panel members included fficers and committee personnel and lay and clergy representatives who took opposing sides on the issue.

Our third step was to select six "model" congregational responses reflecting the entire spectrum from vigorous support

to opposition. Information based on a depth interview sched-
ule was drawn from our reputational elites within the parishes. Approximately twelve interviewees, averaging three
hours per interview, were chosen from each congregation.
Hence some seventy depth interviews comprised the sample
from which data were supplied for our analyses.

It is obvious that the enormous amount of work presup-
posed by this research process is best handled by a team of
collaborators. This study would not be possible without the
dedicated efforts of Russell Galloway and William Eichorn,
both doctoral candidates in the Religion and Society program
of the Graduate Theological Union. While I set up the research design and supervised the study, wrote the Introduction, rewrote and edited the manuscript twice from much
longer versions, and saw it through press, the actual credit for
most of its writing goes to Russell Galloway. Mr. Galloway
wrote the first drafts of all the chapters except Chapters 4 and
6, which were written initially by William Eichorn. All three of
us, however, assume joint responsibility for the book's content.

Finally, a word of appreciation to many individuals who
gave freely of their time and help: Our anonymous panel of
informants, for providing the raw data. Dieter T. Hessel, for
his friendly offices and sympathetic understanding and en-
couragement. The staff of the North Coastal Area who ex-
pedited our study, including J. Davis Illingworth, William R.
Grace, and Don Falkenberg. Also, thanks to Oscar J. Hussel,
of the Board of Christian Education, for his consultative assistance, and to a team of long-suffering typists: Thelma
Furste, Ruby Egnew, Margaret Arms, and Virginia Reed.
Finally, our deepest gratitude to the wives and families at the
Galloway, Eichorn, and Lee households for their endurance
of the trials and tribulations, and no small amount of agony,
involved in the study of church conflict.

R. L.

San Francisco Theological Seminary
San Anselmo, California

Contents

Introduction

"Kilroy was here!" used to be the popular slogan of the 1940's, contends Paul Ylvisaker, former Ford Foundation executive. Today the watchword is, "Alinsky is coming!"

Who is this coming man? Dubbed "professional radical," "slum buster," "rabble-rouser," "friend of the dispossessed," "champion of the powerless," Saul David Alinsky is the explosively controversial organizer of the urban poor and director of the Industrial Areas Foundation.

Our focus in this book is not on Alinsky as such, but rather on the institutional response of church groups to a conflict situation sparked by the prospects of Alinsky's coming. Suffice it to say, then, that Alinsky is the leading proponent of "mass community organization." His usual method is to create "people's organizations" among the dispossessed and deprived so that they might articulate their grievances and have the power to change their circumstances. Alinsky's key approaches center in the use of power and conflict and the recognition of self-interest as a basic motivation. Conflict is frequently induced to serve as a welding agent for group cohesion. Alinsky has been described as a "Jewish agnostic of blunt and often profane manners." In recent years his reputation as a "professional radical" has been exploited by the mass media. Alinsky has a unique ability to disturb the still waters of the racial and economic *status quo*.

Truly the "medium is the message." The news that Alinsky
might be coming to the Bay Area at the invitation of the San
Francisco Presbytery triggered one of the liveliest and most
spirited controversies this judicatory has known. (For the
benefit of non-Presbyterian readers, a "presbytery" is a local-
regional geographical governing body of The United Presbyterian Church U.S.A.) Newspaper coverage and Alinsky's
own antics (such as sending the Mayor of Oakland a diaper)
engendered widespread public interest and attention. Perhaps
never before had so many local congregations, so many lay
leaders, trustees, and deacons of local parishes, and so many
pastors within the presbytery been so deeply and directly
concerned about a social issue that revolved around questions
of poverty, race, inner city, and tactics of community organization.

Simply as an exciting, action-packed episode in the history
of Christianity on the Pacific Slope, the experience is worth
recording and recounting. However, our concerns move beyond the sensational and are surely less ephemeral. What we
have here is a case study par excellence of the anatomy of
church conflict.

Several themes will be coursing their way through these
pages. Perhaps the major motif we seek to illuminate is the
agelong clash between two sources of religious understanding,
two perspectives on the role of religion and the mission of the
church: Is the church to comfort or to challenge, to be a conserving agent of stability or an initiator of change? In a sense
the old dialectic between the priestly and the prophetic, the
"church" and the "sect" (in Troeltschian terms) is again the
drama being performed on a new stage with a new cast of
characters. Actually, though, there are two sets of actors in
our drama of the polarized church. One we may call the de-
votees of "Worldly Christianity" and the other players belong
to what we may designate as "Churchly Christianity." At its
worst, the latter often seems "holier than thou," whereas the
former prides itself on being "worldlier than thou."

This study will highlight the precarious split, if not the impending divorce, between these two factions, each seeking its own justification. Unless the ever-widening gap between them is bridged, unless the antinomies are joined, unless there develops common ground for genuine reconciliation, the very survival of the institutional church is in question. More on the schizophrenic church later!

A second theme that captures our attention in this volume is the dynamics of decision-making. Focus here is on the decision-making processes, especially at the presbytery and local congregational levels. Thus subsequent chapters detail and analyze the chronology of events and the impact of the controversy upon particular congregations while bearing in mind the decision-making focus. Who makes what decisions and in what manner in the midst of conflict situations? These questions will surely be crucial in a future to be filled with conflict.

Of passing interest, we may note that an astute observer of the social scene has compared two surveys of community conflict. Sociologist James S. Coleman analyzed forty cases of community conflict in 1929 and noted that nine of these involved local churches. Then he surveyed forty cases occurring in 1957 and discovered that not a single controversy involved churches. Think of the results if he were to examine the scene a decade later: Milwaukee, Rochester, Chicago, Buffalo, Delano, Selma, Detroit, and a host of other cities serve as reminders that the church has moved into the arena of community conflict. Some would even argue that as yet churches stand at the beginning stages of such involvement and that much more may be expected. How church people make decisions when they confront community crisis is a question we shall explore. Its answers are bound to suggest significant lessons for learning and to present behavioral models for future church conduct and strategy.

A third major concern of our inquiry relates to the nature and function of conflict. It appears that a reappraisal of the consequences of conflict is beginning to emerge. Whereas in

14 THE SCHIZOPHRENIC CHURCH

former periods the consensus among church members was overwhelmingly on the side of harmony, stability, continuity, and order, today the key notions that are gaining ascendancy are: tension, dilemma, power struggle, conflict. The God of harmony has been superseded by the God of conflict. In other words, there has been a discernible shift from exclusive reliance upon patterns of consensus and cooperation to an acceptance of a conflict orientation to achieve a greater measure of justice. If this were not the case, it is doubtful whether the Alinsky controversy would have erupted on the floor of the San Francisco Presbytery.

A long-standing tradition of sociological studies has given attention to those processes and factors which bind individuals and roles together in systems which further and enhance social *order*. Priority has focused upon questions that deal with the maintenance, the ongoing life of a society, the cement that holds diverse institutions together and makes them compatible with one another. These questions naturally are biased in the direction of order, equilibrium, and continuity. Now a new breed of thinkers, drawn to questions about power and social change, are dealing with issues of discontinuity and social conflict. It has become axiomatic according to the sociologist Talcott Parsons' so-called "principle of inertia," that a given procedure or life style will continue unchanged in rate and direction unless impeded or deflected by opposing motivational forces. Hence social change is affected by the exercise of social conflict and by power confrontation. Change may be accelerated by opposition.

Our study will seek to explore the theoretical and practical significance of social conflict for the life and work of the churches. Part Three suggests a revised attitude toward conflict as well as guidelines for the future. If we are to expect more, rather than less, conflict in the future, as already violence mounts and grievances are finding expression in public demonstrations in our city streets and college campuses, if ferment and turmoil are the order of the day, then surely there is hardly a more timely and critical subject than the fuller understanding of church and community conflict.

A reassessment of the nature of conflict, of course, relates to our major theme of the polarized church. What the Alinsky controversy did was to bring to the surface some of the latent issues and tensions that are deep-seated in the life of American churches at large. In a sense the issue transcends the Bay Area, Alinsky, and even the plight of the Negro urban ghetto. The incident is no isolated event in an alluring section of the nation. Rather, the Alinsky controversy is a microcosm of the internal crisis of the polarized church. One faction seeks to relate to the world and is intent upon coping with community conflict and social change. The other side of the polarity seeks to "let the church be the church" in its attention to worship, prayer, and the devotional life, and thus provide comfort and joy and solace to Christian lives.

The split may be further illuminated as follows: In this age of tumultuous transitions, when the pages of history are being turned with reckless speed, the children of Bonhoeffer, the "Worldly Theologians," have rediscovered the world. Worldly Christianity, once considered an underground movement among *avant-garde* Christians, is now riding the saddle and eager to do battle. It has captured the command posts of a significant segment of the churches and denominations in America.

The resurgence of Worldly Christianity means that the dialogue between the church and the world has become the pivotal theological theme of our day. What is capturing the attention of laity and clergy alike, as well as many who remain outside the sanctuary, is the "theology and world" books from the pens of Protestant and Roman Catholic thinkers, such as Harvey Cox, Gibson Winter, Colin Williams, Martin Marty, Peter Berger, Pierre Burton, Peter Riga, Joseph Fichter, Robert Richard, Bernard Haring, Arend van Leeuwen, the Bishops Robinson and Pike, and a host of other lights. We now have a whole cadre of worldly theologians: theologians oriented toward the world, affirming the secular, open to humanity and to a Christian humanism.

Armed with a world-affirming, world-directed theology, an ever-growing corps of laity and clergy are seeking ways of penetrating the structures of society and alleviating its ills through direct action means.

A new stir is in the air that seeks to evade neither power nor conflict. Worldly Christianity argues that to strive for social justice is to be an agent for change within history. In the words of Archbishop William Temple: "Listen to the voice of the wind as it sweeps over the world and stand where you can be caught in its onward rush." Theology cannot afford the luxury of looking the other way by constantly proclaiming a message of changelessness for a world that has faith in flux. Too long, so contends the new breed of worldly theologians, the church has stood by the sidelines instead of being the midwife at the birth of the coming new age.

Meanwhile, as Worldly Christianity gains momentum, a religious "backlash," a countervailing influence has arisen. With profound conviction and a sense of indignant commitment, the forces of Churchly Christianity have assailed the followers of Worldly Christianity. Instead of evangelizing, it is argued, the latter have become evangelized. Instead of combating the powers of secularism, they have become secularized. They have prostituted the legitimate concerns of the church and made of the gospel a political ideology. They have tended to put God on their side of a political issue, so that others who disagree are put in a position of disagreeing not with mere mortals but with God. They have converted "relevance" from a slogan to a God, and they are in danger of being overidentified with the latest and newest cultural fad.

Although we have no intention of lumping him into the camp of Churchly Christianity, nevertheless, James Dittes, highly respected professor at Yale Divinity School, echoes a deep suspicion with this penetrating question:

> We have a right to ask the churches' challengers: Who
> is most guilty of escaping into illusion and irrelevance?
> For there is a grave risk that the seeming "relevance of
> special ventures," such as direct social action *may* be an
> evasion of the responsibility to respond to God in one's
> own station and to set right the affairs of one's own life.
> The great crusade to attack the devil on his home ground
> is particularly alluring and also demonically spurious
> just when the devil is busy in one's own home ground.
> (*The Church in the Way*, pp. 5–6; Charles Scribner's
> Sons, 1967. See also Paul Ramsey, *Who Speaks for the
> Church?* Abingdon Press, 1967.)

Perhaps the easy way out, Dittes suggests, is to press in
public a battle one has abandoned in private. So it is charged
that instead of transforming the world, the followers of
Worldly Christianity have been transformed by it, and, as a
result, the church has become one more community agency
to dispense social welfare. The church has thus lost its dis-
tinctive spiritual, charismatic power to be an agent of reconciliation, a messenger of salvation, proclaiming the crucified
and risen Christ.

Needless to say, there are ancient roots of the religious
polarity we have depicted. Sociological literature is replete
with illustrative findings of this basic tension. The functional
analysis of Émile Durkheim's *Elementary Forms of the
Religious Life*, and more recently, Liston Pope's *Millhands
and Preachers*, Charles Y. Glock's several writings, especially
To Comfort and to Challenge, and Peter Berger's *The Sacred
Canopy*, these and many other studies describe religion as
functioning along lines we have called Churchly Christianity.

It may be instructive to shift the focus away from the immediate, contemporary scene and to view the polarity from
an entirely different cultural and historical perspective. Following Arend van Leeuwen's lead in *Christianity in World
History*, we note a similar tension between the agricultural and
the pastoral settings. Agricultural cultures (notably Egyptian,

Babylonian, and Indian) emerged in the great river valleys (Nile, Tigris and Euphrates, Indus). Their survival depended largely upon control of the rivers. This, in turn, required a highly centralized and bureaucratic social structure. In these cultures, religion served predominantly as social cement and the priesthood was subservient to the political structure. Thus, agricultural civilizations were the chief context for religion as an instrument for conserving the existing patterns of society.

In pastoral cultures, on the other hand, decentralization was the keynote. Pastoral peoples lived in small tribes on the margins of the great agricultural centers. They did not centralize or develop powerful bureaucracies. In some of these cultures, religion was not locked in with the political process. This enabled the religious leaders to exercise a prophetic function. They challenged and criticized the actions of the political power structure. The classic example, of course, was the Hebrew prophets, who confronted and challenged the kings. The same, of course, was true of the early Christians in the Roman Empire. Thus, the Judeo-Christian tradition is characterized by a strong streak of prophetic action. What has happened, however, is that with increasing cultural acceptance Christianity has become accommodated to its culture and has been recruited to play a legitimizing and supportive role similar to that of the ancient agricultural and tribal religions. Nevertheless, the prophetic role remains alive and the institutional church actually becomes its bearer. Hence the saga of the Christian church may be related in one sense as a tension between these two powerful tendencies. This polarity, sometimes creative, sometimes destructive, we submit, is the broader canvas upon which we may paint in more specific strokes the picture of the Alinsky controversy.

PART ONE
THE PRESBYTERY DECISION

1
Countdown on Crisis

BACKGROUND

Whether the San Francisco Presbytery should provide funds to support Saul Alinsky for a community organization program was the question that touched off a major crisis. Before relating the particulars of that crisis, it is necessary to sketch the background situation.

The late fifties and early sixties saw the balance of power of the major Protestant denominations (and more recently the Roman Catholic Church) shift to the social activists. A change in emphasis toward social involvement, propelled by a sense of frustration among many younger clergymen, became dramatically evident in the San Francisco Presbytery. Leaders with conservative leanings were displaced, as the strategy of the "angry young men" to supply more liberal leaders for key staff and committee positions won the day.

While these internal developments occurred, rapid changes in the world at large were ushering in new challenges. Negro migrations from the South to the North and West had given rise to large ghettos and poverty pockets in major industrial centers. In the Bay Area, West Oakland and the Mission District of San Francisco had become festering problem areas.

In 1963, the 175th General Assembly of the United Presbyterian Church responded to issues posed by the civil rights

movement by creating a Commission on Religion and Race
(CORAR). The North Coastal Area of the Synod of California followed suit by setting up its own CORAR. (Since
these events, the tri-presbytery North Coastal Area has been
restructured as the Synod of the Golden Gate.)

Shortly after its founding, CORAR was precipitated into
a crisis, for in that year California faced Proposition 14, the
legislative initiative to repeal the state's "open housing" law.
CORAR became deeply embroiled in the battle. After the
elections of 1964, in which the position advocated by CORAR
on Proposition 14 was decisively defeated, San Francisco
CORAR was dissolved—reputedly in order to allow the
church to recover from the battle. Thus, during the crucial
year of 1965, San Francisco Presbytery was without a special
committee for racial issues. 1965, of course, saw the outburst
of riots throughout the country, most notably in the Watts
section of Los Angeles.

The lack of a formal committee, however, should not be
taken to mean complete inactivity on the race question during
1965. Racial concern, for example, was central for an informal
group of predominantly inner-city pastors who held *ad hoc*
meetings to plan strategy and implement programs directed
against discrimination and poverty. Sometimes referred to as
the "caucus group," this group was ecumenical, but had strong
Presbyterian participation. Concern with mass community organization and Saul Alinsky probably originated within this
group of urban ministers.

ALINSKY AT ASILOMAR

At this point events took a decisive turn. Alinsky was invited to Asilomar—a conference ground in Pacific Grove,
California. From August 30 through September 10, 1965, the
Department of Urban Church sponsored a Seminar on Community Organization as in-service training for urban clergymen. An interdenominational group of roughly forty Bay Area

ministers, including most of the so-called "caucus group," attended the seminar.

Alinsky, as usual, was blunt and forceful. He moved directly to the themes of self-interest, power, conflict, and controversy. Using his Back-of-the-Yards experience in Chicago as his principal illustration, he explained in detail the strategy and tactics of community organization. He stated clearly that the church can be a significant factor in solving poverty problems through community organization. He referred to the Bible as an organizer's manual and to Moses and Paul as two of history's greatest organizers.

The seminar with Alinsky proved to be a potent catalyst. Many of the participants came to appreciate both the need for community organization and the effectiveness of Alinsky's approach. For the members of the "caucus group" this was nothing new: they had been familiar with Alinsky for some time and had wanted to recruit him for a project in the Bay Area. As far as the others are concerned, it is worth noting that Saul Alinsky is a persuasive man. His ability to convey a sense of honesty and responsibility has a way of impressing and converting those with whom he has direct contact. This is particularly significant since personal contact with Alinsky dispels some popular myths that he himself has fostered to increase his tactical effectiveness.

In any case, the effect of the seminar was to solidify and mobilize sentiment in favor of bringing Alinsky and the IAF into the Bay Area. While still at Asilomar, one group of men formed ACTION (Alinsky Committee to Integrate Oakland Now). ACTION was an ecumenical pressure group designed to confront the church power structure and to get Alinsky into Oakland. It seems likely that if those opposed to Alinsky had understood the nature of the group, the issue would have come before the public, and the debate would have been substantially altered. As it happened, however, the *Oakland Tribune* thought the name of the group was Action Committee To Integrate Oakland Now; so they missed the point and the plan remained secret. ACTION has been criticized by one of its own members as pushing a kind of "Alinsky Imperialism": it tried to force an Alinsky package on Oakland without really knowing about the community or taking its uniqueness seriously. In the last analysis, ACTION remained a paper organization which did not take any significant steps on its own.

A group continued to meet after Asilomar, referring to themselves as the "Alinsky Alumni." This group comprised roughly the same men who had formerly been in the caucus group. The effect of the seminar for them was to focus their goal on community organization and the IAF and to increase their insistence on immediate action. Their intention was to find some way to get Alinsky into the Bay Area.

Although a number of solid and powerful Alinsky supporters could now be identified, the institutional channels for obtaining official church action were still unclear.

REACTIVATION OF CORAR

In October, 1965, another important event took place: a national Presbyterian CORAR team visited California and recommended that San Francisco Presbytery's CORAR be reactivated. The team's report emphasized that "the Bay Area has all of the problems plaguing large urban communities that have a large Negro population." Oakland, in particular, was mentioned as a problem center with riot potential. Alinsky and community organization received favorable comment in the report, and the following specific recommendations were made: that CORAR be reestablished and that some aggressive, action program be developed for dealing with minority groups. Members of the North Coastal Area's staff agreed that CORAR would be reactivated to serve as an advocating group with primary emphasis on change and action.

Thus, at the beginning of 1966, San Francisco Presbytery created the institution that was to take over the fight for

Alinsky. The new CORAR included individuals, primarily inner-city pastors and members of the Alinsky Alumni, who were ready to press for action. A dedicated layman and former atomic physicist, Morris J. (Sandy) Sanderson, became director of the program. He had been a member of CORAR and was active in its earlier stand against Proposition 14. He came to San Francisco after acting as temporary director of the newly formed Commission on Church and Race of Southern California, whose efforts focused largely on the problems created by the Watts riot. Sanderson came to San Francisco independently convinced that mass community organization was the best means for redressing Negro grievances. In a letter to a friend he wrote:

> The first thing I would say is that I became "sold" on mass (community) organization as a result of my personal experience in Watts. I could expand on this at considerable length. Suffice it to say that I became aware from a constant listening in the Watts area that the 10's of millions of OEO funds, the heroic work of Chad McClelland in locating nearly 5,000 jobs, the many volunteer services (medical, legal, psychological, educational), etc. were not as effective in changing attitudes as the $150 which Father Samuels, an Episcopalian priest, used in an organizational effort with gang leaders to stop economic exploitation. I am not denying the validity and worth of the other efforts. It is just that I "understand" for the first time what the difference is between doing things for and doing things *with* people.

Sanderson's new position was chief CORAR staff member for the entire North Coastal Area including San Francisco, San Jose, and Redwoods Presbyteries. Significantly, this new group had a clean agenda and was free to concentrate on the Alinsky question.

Events Preceding the April 12 Meeting

By the beginning of 1966, the stage was set for action and reaction. The significant events of this period involve the

activities of (1) CORAR, (2) the Alinsky Alumni, and (3) a
budding opposition to the proposed alliance with Alinsky.
First a brief word about the opposition: nearly all who were
caught up in the early developments were essentially in favor
of Alinsky. Opposition was almost wholly silent and unorganized. Those who later argued against CORAR and
Alinsky recall that they had some indication about the Asilomar conference and that they picked up scuttlebutt about a
possible move for Alinsky. Largely however, the future opponents of Alinsky were almost wholly uninformed about both
Alinsky and the plans to invite him to the Bay Area. One
major exception was Don Buteyn, the Berkeley pastor who
ultimately became the "loyal opposition" and who was responsible for most of the alternative proposals. Buteyn had
attended the Asilomar conference and had even been a
charter member of ACTION. Soon, however, he saw that—
in his words—"Alinsky-type community organization is only
one way to fly and that the church should offer a variety of
possible approaches to the poverty community." Apart from
these sporadic flickers, however, the anti-Alinsky forces were
silent. Only at a later date would a strong opposition become
organized and effective.

When Sanderson came to the San Francisco office in January, he came into close contact with the Alinsky Alumni.
Here, of course, the Alinsky Alumni saw an organizational
channel for pressing their program, but they are eager to have
it understood that no "deals" were made with Sanderson. On
January 18, the Alinsky Alumni met, with Sanderson present,
and drafted a proposal calling for an interfaith religious commitment of $200,000 to support mass community organization.
This document marks the first real embodiment of the proposal that had been in the air since Asilomar and earlier.

In the latter part of January, even before CORAR had
officially begun, Sanderson met with the North Coastal Area's
General Council and requested that the General Councils of
the three presbyteries call emergency meetings to consider a

CORAR proposal on mass community organization. Letters were sent to leading national executives informing them of Sanderson's intentions and asking for reactions. According to Sanderson, the replies were essentially favorable, but they warned the San Francisco officers to solicit ecumenical support and to be prepared for a fight.

During February, San Francisco Presbytery's reactivated CORAR began its official existence. Paul Gertmenian, a respected pastor of an urban residential church, was appointed chairman. From the start the question of community organization dominated the attention of CORAR. The committee members, of course, were not all familiar with the operations of the Industrial Areas Foundation.

The process of educating CORAR was, as the members admit, done hurriedly; the feeling was that the church had waited long enough and that the matter was urgent because of the riot potential in Oakland. This latter suggestion is a rather important feature of the overall picture. During the early part of 1966, the public's attention was drawn to a spate of articles which warned that Oakland was potentially the next Watts. The articles appeared in such notable publications as *Newsweek, The Wall Street Journal, The Christian Century,* and *Ramparts.* Many of the men involved in the events of early 1966 would later look back at the apparent "hurry" of CORAR and say that they were pressured by the threat of a burning, that they were "running scared in front of the shadow of the long, hot summer."

During this period, Presbyterian officials met with Alinsky and discovered that he was interested in plans for community organization in the Bay Area with a budget of approximately $200,000. Thus, as the new chairman of CORAR put it, "At the end of February we got down to business."

During the early part of March, CORAR mailed to all North Coastal Area pastors copies of a Kansas City report favoring Alinsky. Work on the interfaith proposal continued. A group of pro-Alinsky men met to analyze the voting blocs in the presbytery. In Oakland, the Social Education and Action Committee of the Oakland Council of Churches attempted to persuade the Council to adopt an Alinsky program, but the proposal was tabled. During the same period, the General Council of the San Francisco Presbytery was notified that CORAR intended to ask for a special meeting on a proposal to raise $200,000 for community organization.

The next significant event was a "trial run" on March 26 in San Jose Presbytery, the southern member of the tri-presbytery North Coastal Area. A motion was presented in three parts: (1) to make community organization a priority, (2) in conjunction with the other North Coastal Area presbyteries, to raise $200,000 to support the IAF in the Bay Area, (3) to delegate fund-raising responsibilities to CORAR. Consideration of the proposal took roughly four hours. Voting was planned by the Committee on Church and Society only if the situation looked favorable; if not they intended to table the matter for an additional month's education. The committee took a poll of the lunch-time discussion groups and decided to go ahead with the vote. Parts 1 and 3 passed easily, but part 2 yielded a tie vote after an hour and a half's debate. The Moderator broke the tie by voting "no," and the proposal was defeated.

Several lessons were learned from the defeat. Most significantly, CORAR felt that more education about community organization would be necessary before the San Francisco meeting. In addition, it was decided to separate the endorsement of community organization from the call for the IAF and to focus on direct, open floor debate rather than discussion groups.

After the San Jose meeting CORAR was ready to zero in on the April 12 emergency meeting of the San Francisco Presbytery. During March, San Francisco CORAR had moved into action. On March 17, CORAR advised the San Francisco General Council of its intention to make the proposal. On March 25, the General Council agreed to call a special meeting of the presbytery on April 12 to consider the urban situation and specifically the IAF proposal by CORAR. The call included the following statement of purpose:

> Considering and acting upon a course of action responsive to the urban situation in the greater Bay Area, including a proposal for the Commission on Religion and Race to consider community action by the Industrial Areas Foundation headed by Saul Alinsky.

The call for the emergency meeting arrived at most churches on April 1, the Friday before Palm Sunday.

CORAR's strategy at this point was to educate the presbyters by two means. First, CORAR distributed information packages that included "Questions and Answers" about Alinsky and the report of the Kansas City Episcopal Diocese. Second, CORAR held breakfast meetings for clergy and laity. The breakfast meetings were limited in several regards: they were few, they were aimed at individuals considered "open" to the idea, and they were for information and education.

To cite an example, CORAR held a breakfast meeting on April 2 at San Francisco's Calvary Presbyterian Church. Among those present were two laymen who would later become deeply engaged in the controversy. One of them felt that the presentation was too pat to allow for real dialogue. After the meeting when most of the others had gone, the two laymen remained to speak with the CORAR leaders. They strongly counseled CORAR to draw back and not to push the matter, but CORAR felt that it was safe to go ahead and that they could carry the proposal. The laymen, on their own initiative, arranged meetings between CORAR and several of Oakland's Negro leaders. A meeting was held on April 7 at which the Negro leaders expressed reservations about Alinsky. Nevertheless, CORAR's determination was not to be gainsaid.

CORAR's final effort at premeeting education was to bring in John McCrory to address several meetings on April 11. McCrory, a conservative Rochester lawyer, had been hand-picked by CORAR to present the experience of another presbytery and was prepared to testify on the basis of Alinsky's activities in Rochester that the IAF is a responsible and effective organizer. McCrory met with Oakland clergy and laity at a luncheon at Oakland's Athens Club and in the evening at First Presbyterian Church, Oakland.

At this point, it is possible to make some observations about the activities of men who opposed the CORAR proposal. CORAR's adversaries report that they were angry and unorganized. Granted that CORAR's plan had been "in the wind" for some time, these men felt that they had not been informed and that a surprise was being sprung. When one of the most vocal clergy opposition leaders heard from a member of San Jose Presbytery about the action taken there, it seemed to him like "a betrayal that this matter was presented to a geographically remote group before it was even announced in Oakland."

Apart from these spotty indications, the first real notice of CORAR's intent was the official "call" for the special meeting on April 12. The timing infuriated those individuals most strongly opposed to the CORAR proposal and even angered many who would later turn out to be CORAR supporters. With Easter schedules and attitudes prevalent, the clergy generally felt that they could not inform their congregations (or even themselves) on the matter. This timing was later to give rise to much speculation concerning possible CORAR motives to railroad the measure through an unprepared presbytery.

To return to the opposition leader mentioned above, upon receiving the call, he immediately contacted Paul Gertmenian to protest and request a delay. Negotiations were then begun with Don Buteyn to prepare a counterproposal. Buteyn accepted on the condition that the counterproposal be his own work. Buteyn then called Gertmenian and received permission to present his alternative at the April 12 meeting. Although there was some collaboration on this matter, Buteyn did remain in charge of his presentation. Meanwhile, the opposition leader remained active up to the limits of his time

and energy. He presented the matter to the session of his
church and received a strongly negative reaction toward
CORAR's position. On March 30, he requested permission to
distribute a response to CORAR's "Questions and Answers."
While admitting the need for more democratic participation
by Negroes in matters affecting their own destiny, his statement stressed that much progress was already being made
through existing programs and that the Negroes did not want
Alinsky. In addition, he referred to the dubiousness of both
CORAR's and Alinsky's methods. The opposition leader's last
activity before the April 12 meeting was to attend the CORAR
luncheon at the Athens Club on the 11th. His reaction was
anger: this was "the first consultation with Oakland pastors,"
and there was no opportunity for dialogue.

As April 12 approached, the voices calling for delay became
increasingly forceful. Although there was an apparent feeling
within CORAR that the proposal would carry, some concern
about the reaction began to develop. Consequently, the
CORAR leaders agreed with others that they would table the
vote on Item 3, the Alinsky measure, particularly if the emotions of the presbyters were running high.

THE CRISIS: APRIL 12 MEETING

On April 12, 1966, the Tuesday after Easter Sunday, San
Francisco Presbytery had its emergency meeting and thus
initiated what has been called the most intense controversy
in the history of the presbytery. Furthermore, the meeting
itself will in all likelihood be remembered as one of the most
exciting or devastating meetings in presbytery records. Admittedly, the session was not so uproarious as, say, Khru-
shchev's display of shoe-pounding at the United Nations. But
for Presbyterians, with their near obsession for doing things
"decently and in order," this meeting was far from normal.

The meeting was held in Oakland's First United Presbyterian Church at seven thirty in the evening. Despite the general

lack of information about what was to transpire, emotion was running high. Anti-Alinsky literature was distributed in front of the church. The large sanctuary was full. The delegates, mostly pastors accompanied by their ranking elders, were seated in the roped-off front half of the church. The meeting got off to a slow start. Without serious debate or objection, the presbytery approved various requests for other funds amounting to at least $500,000 including $100,000 for a parking lot.

At about nine o'clock, the Commission on Religion and Race took the floor to present its proposal. Paul Gertmenian, the CORAR chairman, offered a four-point motion that the presbytery (1) reaffirm its concern for ethnic and poverty minorities, (2) take action to make available to the poverty communities experienced community organization services, (3) borrow $200,000 to finance two action projects with Alinsky and the Industrial Areas Foundation, (4) appoint a fundraising committee to solicit the $200,000. Items 1, 2, and 4 were not expected to cause much trouble. Item 3 on the other hand, the motion to provide funds for Alinsky, was certain to spark controversy.

After reading the motion, Gertmenian introduced Sanderson, who strongly advocated the proposal. Sanderson was followed by John McCrory, who related his experiences with Alinsky in Rochester; he attempted to dispel the feeling that Alinsky is an evil figure and to indicate that the IAF does operate responsibly. Thus far, the meeting was low-keyed and consistent with CORAR's plans.

After McCrory concluded his remarks, Don Buteyn took the floor. Buteyn presented an alternative proposal for a church-centered community organization to be run by the Oakland Council of Churches at a cost of $30,000 for three years. His main objective was to avoid recommending any particular method for dealing with poverty problems. He felt that presbytery should offer a "menu" of possible solutions to the indigenous community and ask them which they would prefer. Consequently, Buteyn's proposal omitted any reference to the

IAF. This alone was enough to draw the support of those who feared and opposed Alinsky.

Apart from the omission of Alinsky and the IAF, the CORAR forces saw two additional weaknesses in Buteyn's proposal: in the first place, the alternative called for only $30,000 in "seed" money over three years, a figure that CORAR felt would make the entire program ineffective; in the second place, Buteyn's approach called for the action to be initiated and controlled by churches. In short, although Buteyn's proposal appeared fairly progressive on the surface, the liberals felt that its passage would be a complete defeat for CORAR's hopes.

After Buteyn finished reading his alternative proposal, the plot began to thicken. The CORAR tacticians were surprised by a motion from the floor that the alternative proposal be substituted for item 3 of the CORAR proposal. The motion was seconded, and the alternative was on the floor for consideration. The debate that ensued has been characterized as the most intense in the history of the presbytery. Impassioned speeches were delivered by factions ranging from reactionary to radical. Opinion varied from the view that Alinsky was in league with the forces of hell to the view that anything other than Alinsky would be like putting a band-aid on a cancer. After an hour or more of debate, the question was called, and the alternative proposal was defeated by roughly sixty votes.

The defeat of the alternative put item 3 back on the floor. Delegates leaped to their feet and shouted for the floor. Others rushed down the aisles to the front of the church to demand recognition. On the platform, hurried negotiations ensued. The focus of the matter was this: Sanderson and Gertmenian had, before the meeting and under pressure from those who wanted more time, entered into some sort of agreement to table item 3. The idea was to allow another month's discussion and education before a final vote. What happened on the platform during this period is not clear. One version is that Sanderson passed the word to Buteyn to make a mo-

tion to table item 3, but Buteyn said he had had a fair hearing and had no desire to table the motion. Buteyn's version is
that he did try to make the tabling motion but that he failed
to get the Moderator's attention in time. Another feeling is
that the CORAR leaders, guessing that they could gain approval of item 3 by a narrow vote, simply backed out on their
agreement. (One important layman resigned from CORAR
over this matter.)

In any case, the plan to table the motion had a fatal blow.
The Moderator was trying to recognize those who had not
spoken before. Thus even if Buteyn had been trying to get the
floor, there was almost no chance of his being recognized.
Amid the pandemonium, the chair recognized another delegate who called for a vote on item 3. The clerk ruled that the
call for the vote ended the debate. Dr. Baird requested prayer
before the vote, but he was shouted down. Thus, without any
direct debate on the item, the fateful vote was held, and item
3 passed 107–88 with twelve abstentions. San Francisco Presbytery had voted to provide $200,000 for community organiza-
tion under Saul Alinsky.

Before passing on to the aftermath of April 12, we should
mention two final matters. There is a difference of opinion
about the amount of calculated strategy that went into the
narrow CORAR victory. According to Presbyterian rules, the
committee calling a special meeting has the prerogative to
set up the general plan for the session. CORAR used this opportunity to get the first three slots including a place for
McCrory. Apart from that, little is clear. Some say that there
were fairly sophisticated polls taken indicating that CORAR
would win narrowly. On the other hand, many on both sides
of the issue were surprised that the proposal passed.

A bone of contention that persisted after the meeting was
the treatment of opposition speakers. Recall that those opposed
to the action felt they had received such short notice that they
had not been able to prepare for proper rebuttal. In addition,
however, a number of the opposition speakers felt that they

were not even given time to *present* their arguments. Statements were limited to five minutes. The leader of the opposition in the Peninsula, among others, was abruptly cut off in the middle of his remarks. One opposition pastor attempted to play a tape recording made in Rochester and was ruled out of order. Thus, the opposition felt that the meeting itself was designed and carried out with the intention of denying a fair hearing to those who opposed CORAR's plan.

2

Reaction to the Action

CORAR leaders were surprised by the intensity of feelings expressed at the April 12 meeting. Some could see the writing on the wall even before the meeting adjourned and knew that CORAR was in for more than it had bargained for. Many delegates, although displeased with both the content and the method of CORAR's action, went home assuming that the matter was settled. No immediate protest was evident. Some men even phoned the CORAR office and assured the staff of their intention to support implementation despite their unhappiness with the decision.

The event that lighted the fuse of reaction came two days later. An article in the April 14 edition of the *Oakland Tribune* gave fourteen columns to the presbytery action. The tenor of the article was consistent with the newspaper's conservative image. It began as follows: "He is a professional radical, an organizer of the poor, an agitator who seeks to rub raw the sores of discontent." Carefully citing Alinsky's own words, the article then related a "parade of horrors" designed to terrify even the most complacent. Revolution, hate and violence, battles against City Hall and the fat cats, death watches— these are just a few of the warnings mentioned. Opinions were culled linking Alinsky with the Communists. In short,

Tribune article predicted disaster of the highest order if Presbyterians succeeded in their intention to impose Alinsky upon Oakland. This was followed by an article in the *San Francisco Chronicle* entitled "Alinsky's Coming and the Fur Flies" and by a week's front-page coverage in various Bay Area newspapers. The most significant aspect of the newspaper coverage was that many Presbyterian laymen in the Bay Area received their *first introduction* to Saul Alinsky through the *Tribune*. They had not been informed about Alinsky and the action to be taken, and when they saw the opinion of Oakland's mayor that Alinsky would produce only hate, anger, and divisiveness, they panicked.

Although a complete annotation of the reaction is impossible, a few developments may be cited to indicate the intensity of response. A systematic telephone campaign was begun to encourage members to withdraw pledges from churches. Similarly, a letter campaign was carried out, and petitions circulated. Churches threatened to withdraw funds from national Presbyterian projects. The press coverage continued to whip up sentiment. The Oakland City Council passed a resolution declaring Alinsky *persona non grata* in Oakland. Leaders of presbytery, of the Negro community, and of the San Francisco antipoverty program came out against Alinsky. The opposition within the presbytery, particularly among the laity, began to organize and to exert heavy pressure. Within ten days, formal protests were received from at least fifteen churches. During this period, Illingworth received roughly fifty letters, nine tenths of which were against the presbytery action.

Meanwhile, the anti-Alinsky position was given formal statement by attorneys for the Presbyterian Committee for Study and Action, a newly formed opposition group known publicly as the Ad Hoc Appeals Committee. Documents were drafted which included a Notice of Appeal and Request for Stay of Proceedings and a brief which listed the following grounds of appeal: irregularity of proceedings; lack of indulgence for those speaking against the proposal at the April 12 meeting; admission of improper testimony, haste, prejudice, and mistake. The brief also pointed out the failure of CORAR to communicate properly with church members:

> Appellant is informed and believes that the failure of CORAR to communicate its proposal "to the several congregations" is the root problem out of which has arisen the basic schism and conflict facing the church today. (Brief, p. 4.)

In short, CORAR found itself embroiled in controversy and under attack from almost every direction. The first phase of CORAR's response was to "stand pat and educate." This phase was to last until the tri-presbytery meeting on April 26. At this point, there seems to have been a growing recognition on the part of the CORAR leaders that the lesson of San Jose Presbytery had not been adequately learned, that even more educating should have been done prior to the decision. Nevertheless, CORAR did have a decision in its favor, and the feeling was that they could stick it out and weather the storm through after-the-fact education.

CORAR leaders began to prepare a campaign designed to justify the decision in the minds of Presbyterians by educating them on the virtues of Alinsky and community organization. The first tactic was to invite Presbyterians to "area meetings" at which CORAR would present the pros and cons of community organization. The second tactic was to prepare more substantial information packages for distribution. The third tactic was to use the forum offered by the tri-presbytery meeting scheduled for April 26 in order to present a "clarifying statement."

Thus, despite the intensity of the public reaction, CORAR approached the tri-presbytery meeting—as Gertmenian put it—"hoping for reconciliation." CORAR's plan was to distribute its package of documents, to explain the coming area meetings, and then to offer its clarifying statement. At the meeting itself, however, CORAR found unabated hostility. In a parliamentary political move, the opposition used an "order of the day" motion to stop debate on whether CORAR's clarifying statement should be accepted. The meeting was ultimately adjourned without any action taken on the CORAR offer of clarification. Thus, the tri-presbytery meeting, instead of providing conciliation, revealed the depth and intensity of the split within presbytery. To quote a CORAR leader: "By April 26, chaos prevailed, that's the best word for it."

To what degree was CORAR's opposition organized during the period from April 12 to April 26? Apart from the general wave of public reaction and sporadic volleys by scattered quasi-organizations and individuals, the Ad Hoc Appeals Committee was the one major group of anti-CORAR Presbyterians who organized into a fairly effective pressure group. The committee had its initial meeting at Loveley's Restaurant in Oakland, where a predominantly lay assemblage voiced its intention to force a hearing in their churches and a rehearing at presbytery level. From this beginning, the group expanded to include one hundred eighty-six individuals from eighteen churches. Although a few clergymen played significant roles, the group remained essentially a lay organization. As stated by one of its leaders, an Oakland lawyer, the reasons for the group's position were resistance to the man Alinsky—his style, his tactics, his results—and resistance to the notion that the church should be so deeply involved in society. A few, of course, wanted no action at all, but the majority sought reconsideration and substitution of a more palatable alternative. The Ad Hoc Appeals Committee was a self-financed, grassroots organization that placed predominant emphasis on teaching. During the period in question, April 12 to 26, the most notable activity of the group was to draw up appeal documents and to hold breakfast meetings for education and planning.

APRIL 26 TO JUNE 7: EFFORTS AT EDUCATION

The tri-presbytery meeting on April 26 made it plain that CORAR's intention to stand pat and educate was insufficient to deal with the crisis at hand. Press coverage continued to keep tempers aroused. Nearly twenty formal protests and requests for reconsideration, representing some of the most powerful churches within the presbytery, had been received. The Oakland Council of Churches had taken the motion for an Alinsky program off the table and, after heated debate, defeated it. Alinsky had made the matter even tougher by sending the Mayor of Oakland a set of diapers with appropriate commentary and thereby had thrown the members of various churches into a "blue panic," as the chairman of Redwoods CORAR put it. The chaos at the tri-presbytery meeting indicated finally that conciliatory action was needed.

On April 28, San Francisco Presbytery's General Council took action to ease the tension. The meeting, lasting from noon until 5:00 P.M., began with a report on the many notices of intent to move for reconsideration. CORAR felt, and apparently the General Council agreed, that the requests for reconsideration were not procedurally valid: they were all filed by churches voting against the CORAR proposal, rather than in the affirmative (a requirement for requesting reconsideration). Although CORAR felt no legal compulsion, the leaders did sense by now that something was needed. Consequently, they were ready to go along with the suggestions of the General Council. According to one of its members, the consensus of the General Council was that there had been severe polarization and that "we needed to restore amity."

Toward this end, the General Council decided to invoke a device that has venerable precedent among Presbyterians: to call a blue ribbon bipartisan committee. To state the matter more systematically, the decision of the General Council was fourfold: to move to reconsider item 3 on June 7, to ask CORAR to take no implementing action under the April 12 decision until then, to appoint a bipartisan committee, and to have the committee report on June 7 as part of the debate on reconsideration. The bipartisan committee was chartered to "evaluate the Industrial Area Foundation and possible alternatives to Item 3." After brainstorming for names, the Council made its selection of committee members on two criteria, moderation and representation of all sides of the debate.

CORAR agreed to the requests of the General Council. For a while CORAR considered a floor fight over the selection of committee members, but then it decided to acquiesce. CORAR did not consider the action as a "backing away" by the General Council from its formerly favorable position. Rather, the decision was seen merely as an attempt to restore unity and peace and reason. CORAR accepted the suggested reconsideration because, as Gertmenian put it, "Our feeling was that we could hold the line."

With the appointment of the bipartisan committee and the request that CORAR withhold any action to implement the earlier decision, tempers began to cool and a period of education began. Several factors aided in de-escalating the crisis. Press coverage finally dropped off, thus canceling one of the most inflammatory forces in the controversy. An outspoken member of the anti-Alinsky faction was called before a judicial committee to answer charges stemming from his statements that CORAR officials were on the payroll of the IAF and had attempted to bribe a trustee of presbytery; the individual retracted his statements and issued an apology. The decisive event for the easing of tensions, however, was the San Francisco Presbytery meeting on May 10, at which the General Council announced its decisions. General Council and CORAR had promised the San Francisco clergy that no action concerning Alinsky would be taken at this meeting, but doubts ran high. Thus, when the meeting went by without incident, individuals around the Bay Area began to relax. It was during the subsequent period from May 10 to June 7 that, as the Stated Clerk reported, the presbytery finally tried to grapple with the issues involved in the controversy. During this time, education proceeded in three important channels: the bipartisan committee, the CORAR area meetings, and the breakfast meetings held by the Ad Hoc Appeals Committee.

The Bipartisan Committee. When the General Council of San Francisco Presbytery decided to call a bipartisan committee "to evaluate the Industrial Areas Foundation and possible alternatives to item 3," it was relying on venerable precedent and resorting to a classic maneuver in conflict resolution.

What was the composition of the committee? Four clergymen and seven laymen were chosen for the eleven-member committee. Two Negro laymen and two CORAR representatives were among the members, and selection was made to ensure representation of both the East and the West Bay. The Hon. Spurgeon Avakian, a distinguished and respected East Bay judge, acted as chairman. It appears that three criteria determined the selection of committee members: representation of all sides of the controversy, ability to command respect, and moderation.

Between May 5 and June 7, the committee met eight times. The goal of the chairman was to avoid premature polarization and commitment, to preserve objectivity and respect, and to focus the early meetings on education while holding off any decision until the last two meetings. Thus, the chairman planned an essentially two-phase deliberation: six meetings for the gathering of information and two meetings for reaching decisions and formulating a report. In retrospect, however, it may be more accurate to subdivide the activities of the committee into three stages: (1) confrontation, (2) education, and (3) decision.

The first two meetings were given over to introduction and confrontation. Each member was requested to introduce himself and give a statement of his biases on the matter at hand. During this early phase there was some direct clash of opposing viewpoints and tempers flared from time to time, but the rough waters were negotiated and the committee came through the crucial period without irreconcilable division. During the first two meetings, the committee appears to have reached consensus on the following matters: that *drastic* action was needed in order to deal effectively with the problems of the poverty communities in the Bay Area, that real progress depended upon changing the underlying *attitudes* of the poor toward their own plight, that the church *must* help to instigate some action, that the *minimum* response would call for some form of community organization and that the *indigenous community* should have the decisive choice in the matter.

Reactions to Alinsky, however, revealed no such consensus. Those opposing CORAR's action argued that the IAF had no clear goal for using the power it developed, that Alinsky's tactics were not based on love, that the committee had insufficient information, and that other approaches were better. The pro-CORAR, pro-Alinsky faction responded that the key to progress in poverty problems is attitudes, not specific goals, that the "brotherly love" approach had not worked, that more information should be disseminated, and that there are, in fact, other good programs. CORAR's strategy, however, was to emphasize that the IAF was in a class by itself in community organization. Phase one in retrospect appears to have been a vigorous exchange of basic ideas.

At the same time, the first two meetings laid the groundwork for phase two, the process of education. In determining how the committee should pursue its purpose, it was decided to have a subcommittee gather and distribute pertinent literature, to encourage members to meet with as many interested parties as possible and to attend the meetings held by CORAR and opposition groups, to invite the Ad Hoc Appeals Committee to present their position, to meet with Alinsky, and to engage in field observation of IAF projects in Chicago, Kansas City, and elsewhere. During this second phase, the attention of the committee gradually shifted from Alinsky to the needs of the community.

Phase two, the educational process, began in earnest at the committee's third meeting when the Ad Hoc Appeals Committee presented its alternative proposal. The predominant feature of the alternative, as in the April 12 meeting, still concerned the role of the church as instigator of community organization. The Ad Hoc group wanted the church to take a more active role: Christian leaders were to be sought; the people's congress was to be called by church leaders; Presbyterians were to be included on the board of directors; the Presbyterian directors were to make reports to the church and request funds. This raised the suspicion in the minds of some committee members that the Ad Hoc group wanted a paternalistic, church-controlled operation rather than a truly indigenous community organization. When challenged as to what they would do if the poverty community requested Alinsky, the representatives of the Ad Hoc group apparently hedged sufficiently to undermine the confidence of the committee. Another problem with the alternative proposal was that its program was goal-directed rather than attitudinal, and this ran counter to one of the committee's earliest conclusions.

During the ensuing three meetings, as one member stated, the committee "got down to the nitty-gritty." Two decisive events were involved in the educational process: field study of IAF projects in other cities and a meeting with Alinsky in Carmel. Three members visited IAF projects while taking trips for other purposes, and one member was sent out on a special trip to Chicago on the committee's behalf. The experiences of the members in the field and the reports given upon their return were a decisive turning point. Perhaps the most significant report came from the two members who observed the Woodlawn Organization in Chicago. For one member, a Negro woman and CORAR member, the visit merely corroborated prior expectations. For the other Woodlawn visitor the Chicago experience comprised a major metamorphosis. This man had been chosen originally to represent the anti-CORAR side of the controversy and had, in fact, been quoted in the newspapers as opposing Alinsky. He had also been one of the charter members of the Ad Hoc Appeals Committee. Although his visit in Woodlawn left some doubt about the long-range effectiveness of the IAF's approach, he came back convinced that the IAF had achieved significant results in Woodlawn, particularly by creating a "sense of accomplishment" within the poverty community. The overall effect of the reports was highly significant. They dispelled the notion that Alinsky's operations are irresponsible, and they led to the firm decision that Alinsky is the most effective community organizer. As one originally anti-Alinsky committee member put it, "No one holds a candle to Alinsky—that's what the committee soon found out."

The second significant event during this period was the committee's meeting with Saul Alinsky in Carmel. To a great extent, Alinsky's public image as an Antichrist has been purposely fostered for its political effectiveness. In person, however, Alinsky impresses many people as a warm, sincere, responsible individual who has a deep and genuine concern for the poor. By meeting with the committee, Alinsky was able to dispel some of the image created by the *Oakland Tribune* and his television appearance.

During this same period, education continued through the other channels opened up by the committee as well. Much pertinent literature was xeroxed and distributed to members. Individual members attended breakfast meetings held both by CORAR and the Ad Hoc Appeals Committee, and consulted with a number of interested participants and churchmen. Of all these matters, however, it has been suggested that "the key seemed to be the actual chance to visit with the people."

The period of intense education set the stage for the third phase in the committee's work, the making of the decision and the formulation of a report. According to committee members, it was understood at a fairly early date that Alinsky was the master of community organization. On the other hand, an

emerging consensus held that the choice of community organization was a matter for the indigenous members of the
poverty communities. Furthermore, there was the strong concern for the unity of the presbytery.

With these factors in mind, the committee approached the
time when a report was called for. At this time, there seems to
have been a 3 (pro)—5 (neutral)—3 (anti) alignment. For a
while, the committee considered requesting additional time
for evaluating alternatives to the IAF and for preparing a
report. In the light of the decision that evaluation of alternatives was essentially a matter for the poverty community itself,
however, the committee decided to go ahead and attempt to
formulate a report. A first draft report prepared by the chairman was acceptable to the center coalition of five, but not
acceptable to either of the three-member coalitions on the
left and right. Thus, during the final two meetings, the committee settled down to debate the decision.

At this point, two controversial issues surfaced. The first
was the treatment of Alinsky and the IAF. CORAR members
continued to press for item 3 as it originally stood, i.e., spe-
cifying support for Alinsky. The majority of the committee,
however, felt that Alinsky should be commended, but that
item 3 should omit specific reference to the IAF and leave the
decision in the hands of the poverty communities. This issue
clearly represents the most difficult matter faced by the committee. Several of the members felt that the situation resolved
itself into a confrontation between a small CORAR faction
and a small anti-CORAR faction. The neutrals, wanting a
unanimous report in order to ensure reconciliation of presbytery, felt that the name should be omitted and persuaded
the pro-CORAR faction to join in. For those who wanted
Alinsky to come into the Bay Area, the idea was that a report
affirming community organization and recognizing Alinsky
as the "only" effective organizer would allow CORAR to implement its intentions. *This was viewed as a risk that had to*

*be taken in order to avoid a minority report that might exacer-
bate the conflict within the presbytery at large.*

The second issue that divided the committee was the delegation of responsibility for determining what the indigenous
community wanted. Anti-Alinsky forces wanted to avoid giving CORAR a carte blanche to invite Alinsky, while the
CORAR forces wanted to avoid the possibility of opening the
issue again before the entire presbytery.

Ultimately compromise was achieved, and a unanimous
decision was reached on the following recommendations:

The committee recommends that the language of resolution no. 3 be amended to read as follows and that, as so
amended, resolution no. 3 be adopted:
It is moved that to implement resolutions nos. 1 and 2
adopted by this presbytery on April 12, 1966, this presbytery:
a. Authorize the borrowing of up to $200,000 in order to
provide funds for the establishment and implementation
of community organization action projects in the San
Francisco Bay Area, subject to approval by the General
Council of Presbytery of a suitable plan of repayment,
and on the condition that any such projects can be undertaken only upon invitation of the people indigenous to
the poverty community areas in accordance with the
methods and procedures established pursuant to the succeeding paragraphs of this motion;
b. Instruct the Commission on Religion and Race
(CORAR) to recommend to the General Council the
procedures by which the people indigenous to the poverty community areas shall themselves decide demo-
cratically what, if any, community organization services
they desire;
c. Instruct CORAR to recommend to the General Council the methods of responding to requests from such poverty community areas for community organization
services;
d. Instruct CORAR to seek a broad ecumenical and
community base of support, financial and otherwise, for
this program to help the poor and oppressed to help

themselves, with the understanding that such fund raising shall be conducted with great sensitivity to the
denominational program of the $50,000,000 fund cam-
paign, as already stated in resolution no. 3 adopted by
this presbytery on April 12, 1966; and
e. Authorize the General Council to take action on behalf of presbytery in implementing the matters covered
in paragraphs a., b., c. and d.

The committee's report also included a discussion of the
general issues faced by the committee, the nature of the committee's deliberations, the committee's conclusions concerning the IAF, other organizations, and the proposal of the Ad
Hoc group, and a general interpretation of the recommendations. As to Alinsky and the IAF, the committee stated:

To use our own words, we do not view Mr. Alinsky as
either a Messiah or a Devil. The IAF is in a class of its
own in the field of mass community organization, simply
because no other organization has attempted to engage in
community organization programs on any comparable
scale. It does not have a record of 100 percent success,
but its batting average cannot be discounted. Whether
the community organizations it has helped to create have
achieved tangible goals is the kind of question which is
always open to debate. Suffice it to say that if community
is itself a desirable goal in areas of economic poverty and
social discrimination, the record of the IAF justifies consideration of it as a possible organizing agency.

Regarding alternatives, the committee was careful to note
the distinction between "community organization" and the
"goal-oriented approaches" that seek to deal with symptoms
rather than underlying causes. After dealing with the Ad Hoc
proposal, the report warned of the danger of paternalism. The
committee then stated its conclusion that "the church's commitment to overcome social injustice in our society can best
be served in the area of community organization by providing
financial assistance to projects which truly represent the de-
cisional judgment of the poverty communities." Thus the
CORAR motion should be modified so as not to mention

"either by inclusion or exclusion what organizational agency may or may not be used."

An additional word of clarification and interpretation is needed at this point. One of the most significant substantive conclusions reached by the committee concerns the endorsement of community organization as opposed to goal-directed programs. As we have said, the crux of the matter is that community organization addresses itself to changing the attitudes of people in the poverty communities. As the report states, the problem of the American Negro is not a mere matter of lack of material resources.

An effective approach to the problem presupposes some means for combating the apathy and low self-esteem that have become prevalent among Negroes. According to the report, this must come by enabling Negroes to participate in their own decisions, and more importantly, to *see* the effects of their participation, to know that their own actions *can* affect their destiny.

In short, after eight meetings lasting more than forty hours and after a substantial amount of inquiry, the bipartisan committee had come up with a compromise report affirming the earlier action to the extent that it sought community organization and endorsed Alinsky as a candidate, but modifying the earlier action by striking the exclusive reference to Alinsky and the IAF. It appears that the chairman was successful in his attempt to maintain order and respect.

As far as the intended consequences of the report and recommendations were concerned, committee members differed. Those favoring CORAR's proposal and Alinsky saw the decision as a necessary compromise designed to pacify Presbytery and still allow CORAR to invite Alinsky. Those skeptical about Alinsky hoped that the modification would at least slow down the activities of CORAR, and perhaps even amount to a *de facto* defeat of CORAR's efforts to bring in the IAF. The neutrals were concerned to avoid paternalism but were leaning in the direction of favoring Alinsky if he were invited by the indigenous community. And, of course, all the members were concerned with bringing in a report which would reconcile presbytery and restore order and amity to the ranks.

CORAR Area Meetings. During the same period in which the bipartisan committee was carrying on its deliberations, education proceeded through other channels. One such channel was the CORAR "area meeting" program. As we have said, when the General Council called the bipartisan committee into existence, it asked CORAR to refrain from implementing the April 12 decision. The idea was to let tensions cool until the June 7 meeting when the committee would bring in its report and the presbytery would reconsider item 3. During May, particularly after the reassuring May 10 presbytery meeting and the fading of press coverage, the presbytery regained a certain amount of composure, and the stage was set for education.

CORAR's attempts to educate the presbytery were twofold: the distribution of a large information package and the holding of area meetings. The package of materials contained information concerning community organization, the IAF, the April 12 meeting, and pertinent bibliography. These materials were distributed to all pastors and elders in the presbytery. In addition, the package of materials contained a letter announcing six area meetings to discuss the issues; later the number of meetings was expanded to fifteen. Both sides of the controversy were heard at these meetings. CORAR, through a representative, began the meeting with an explanation of community organization and the IAF. Then followed an opposition argument by a representative of the opposition group. Attendance at the meetings totalled an estimated 3,000 to 5,000 individuals.

CORAR's chairman has emphasized the amount of education that took place at these meetings, more—he says—than at any other time in recent church history. The Stated Clerk of the presbytery also praised the educational significance of these meetings: "Here presbytery finally came to grips with the issue." Naturally, appraisals of the meetings vary. The general feeling was that the meetings were "fair" and that a reasonably accurate picture was given. Some of the opposition, however, felt that the meetings were nothing more than harangues by CORAR. In any case, there seems to be little doubt that the meetings had an impact on those in attendance. In these CORAR meetings, the people who had had no exposure to the matters at hand, except through the inflammatory reports in the Oakland press, were able to raise questions and to discuss issues.

According to Sanderson's records, the questions asked by the participants clustered on the following points: objections to community organization, objections to the church's seeking outside help rather than organizing on its own, requests for information about the operations of the IAF, objections to Alinsky's atheism, profanity, and use of conflict, and so on. Just as the encounter with the "facts" about Alinsky had substantially changed the attitude of many members of the bipartisan committee, the confrontation at the area meetings served to dispel some of the unfavorable "myths" that had grown up around the name Alinsky and the idea of community organization. By and large, the CORAR leaders felt that the meetings were a success and that those who attended learned that the proposal—and consequently the prior action of CORAR and the presbytery—was not so bad after all. According to Sanderson, "This was the greatest educational experience this Presbytery has ever had."

Ad Hoc Appeals Committee Breakfast Meetings. During these same "days of education," the issues concerning community organization and Alinsky were presented through a third significant channel, namely, the Ad Hoc Appeals Committee (the Presbyterian Committee for Study and Action). In some ways, this third channel represents the most interesting type of response since it involves spontaneous nonestablishment education. Recall that the Ad Hoc Appeals Committee was an essentially lay group that sprang up in the

East Bay in response to the CORAR action of April 12. The group, involving 186 clergy and laity from eighteen different churches, began by challenging both substantively (opposition to Alinsky and community organization) and procedurally (anger concerning what was felt to be a violation of trust by the clergy to inform the laity of the presbytery) the action that had been taken. Thus, the early activities focused on preparing appeals and mobilizing protests and sanctions.

Shortly thereafter, however, the Ad Hoc Appeals Committee began an educational effort paralleling CORAR's. (In fact, one member of the group opined that the CORAR area meetings represent a response to the effectiveness of the Ad Hoc program.) From April until June, the Ad Hoc group held "breakfast meetings" on Saturday mornings. Again, as in the case of the CORAR area meetings, opinion varies concerning the nature and effectiveness of the meetings. CORAR leaders attended a few of the meetings and concluded that they were no threat: the general tone of the meetings was, in their opinion, sufficiently irrational and ineffectual as to render the meetings worthless. According to the leaders of the Ad Hoc Committee, on the other hand, the meetings were reasonable and valuable. One leader stated, "Our emphasis was on teaching." The goal was to present a balanced point of view covering Alinsky and alternatives. No doubt the discussion of Alinsky focused predominantly on how to get rid of him, but the consideration of alternatives appears to have been responsible and serious. Some of the Ad Hoc group, of course, were opposed to any kind of action, but they were not considered to be at the heart of the group. For most of the group, the encounter with the CORAR proposal raised in an unusually powerful way the question of how to deal with the poverty communities. In the process of coping with CORAR, the group was forced to take the problems seriously and to come up with some promising alternatives to Alinsky and community organization. At a later point we will deal with some of the benefits that "spun off" from the controversy. Suffice it to say at this point that the education undertaken by the Ad Hoc Appeals Committee at their breakfast meetings significantly introduced the members of the group to poverty problems, community organization, Alinsky, possible alternatives, and the issue of church involvement.

To recapitulate, the month of May was a time of educational effort for the presbytery. After the tri-presbytery meeting of April 26, the crisis had passed its high point and begun to fade. By this time, press coverage had begun to cool off. Thus, when the General Council called the bipartisan committee to act as guide in a reconsideration of the controversial item 3, Presbyterians began to feel that the immediate pressure was off and that there was time to reason and to be informed. Education during the ensuing month went forward along three predominant routes: within the bipartisan committee, through CORAR information packets and area meetings, and through breakfast meetings held by the Ad Hoc Appeals Committee. With the relaxing of tensions, opinion began to shift. Apart from the educational activities mentioned, action on the issue was at a lower ebb than during the critical period in April. The remaining question, then, was the reconsideration called for by the General Council. Would the presbytery break out into open conflict again? Would the report of the bipartisan committee suffice to resolve the remaining tensions and smooth the way to a reconciled decision? All this hinged on the crucial meeting of June 7.

THE "RESOLUTION"

The June 7 Meeting. The June 7 meeting of San Francisco Presbytery at First Presbyterian Church, Berkeley, was for some a glorious culmination, for some a boring anticlimax, and for others a classic evasion. There can be no doubt that interest still ran high: instead of the normal 225 persons in attendance, there were more than 1,000 delegates and spectators. Having anticipated the turnout, presbytery leaders planned the meeting carefully. Microphones were installed to handle questions and debate. The order of the day was postponed until after dinner to allow all elders to attend. The chair was advised to alternate the debate and to use a written ballot if a division were called for. Finally, it was decided to withhold publication of the committee's report until after dinner. Despite the massive turnout, the temper of the audience was relatively subdued. Perhaps the fact that the committee report had been kept secret contributed to the calmness.

After dinner, the chairman of the General Council moved for reconsideration of the April 12 action, and the motion was carried. The chairman then introduced Judge Spurgeon Avakian, the chairman of the bipartisan committee, who was to announce the committee report. Avakian, in turn, introduced the committee members and then read the entire six-page report aloud. There followed nearly two hours of discussion in which Avakian responded to questions from the floor. The way Judge Avakian handled the discussion has earned him the respect of nearly all concerned persons, pro or con. Apart from a few outbursts, the tone of the discussion was rational and low-keyed. Apparently, many of the previously vocal opposition could see the writing on the wall and took moderate positions.

After the discussion the matter came on for vote. The committee's report represented a compromise position. It supported the April 12 action in affirming concern for poverty communities, in ratifying community organization, in calling for the presbytery to raise $200,000 to support action programs, and in commending Alinsky and the IAF as able and experienced community organizers. It deviated from the April 12 action primarily by striking the specific motion to call Alinsky and substituting a motion to support any organization requested by a representative group of the indigenous population of the poverty communities. At the conclusion of the discussion, the presbytery took four votes. The first was to deny by a two to one majority a substitute motion which would have made presbytery rather than CORAR responsible for implementing the proposal. The second was to deny by a three to one majority an amendment which would have forbade the indigenous community to invite the IAF and receive presbytery money. The third was the vote on the committee's recommendations on a motion by Dr. Carl Howie. Presbytery passed the motion by an overwhelming voice vote with an estimated twenty dissenters. Finally, just before adjournment an opposition leader moved that CORAR be expanded to include more representation of the larger suburban parishes. This motion was referred to the General Council for further consideration.

Although the meeting went smoothly and culminated in an almost unanimous vote in favor of the committee's recommendations, it should not be inferred that satisfaction reigned in all quarters. In fact, reactions varied over an enormous spectrum. Undoubtedly most of those in attendance felt that the meeting had been quite impressive and successful. At the meeting itself, Dr. Illingworth announced that he considered it to be the finest presbytery meeting he had ever seen. Sanderson called it a "glorious meeting." The Stated Clerk said it was "something to behold." And the chairman of Redwoods CORAR called it a "classic case of conflict resolution."

There was, on the other hand, dissent from this favorable evaluation. One pastor remarked, "Many of us felt that the whole thing was so manipulated that we could not bring the matter to a square issue." By using the bipartisan committee, CORAR "bypassed the presbytery and avoided the vote that they would have lost." This opinion was seconded by a leading member of the lay opposition who felt that the June 7 meeting was pure conflict resolution, that it did not deal with the substance of the dispute at all and that it amounted to an admission that the arguments of the "appellants" had not even been considered.

The June 7 meeting may be viewed as the end of the most intense phase of the conflict over CORAR's April 12 proposal. Through various types of conflict resolution including meetings and discussion, distribution of printed materials, the calling of the bipartisan committee and so on, the presbytery succeeded in restoring at least surface calm to its troubled waters.

Interpretations of the June 7 Action. The question of the overall effect of the events occurring between March and June of 1966 will be probed in subsequent chapters. Now we need to sort out and interpret the action taken at the June 7 meeting.

What did the bipartisan committee report actually decide as to the substantive issues involved? What, according to the different factions, was the nature and effect of the committee's modifications of the presbytery's April 12 action? We will consider the opinions of five different elements: the pro-CORAR group, the bipartisan committee moderates, the moderate opposition, the informed anti-Alinsky group, and the most extreme opposition. The CORAR forces to a man considered the committee recommendations to be a victory. In the first place, they felt that the report vindicated the substance of the April 12 action: after all, it called for community organization and singled out Alinsky and the IAF as "one" able organizer. In the second place, they felt that they could "work within the Report." As Gertmenian put it, "We thought we could get Alinsky under the call provision." The moderates on the committee seem to have been controlled by two major considerations: first and foremost, the concern to restore the unity and amity of presbytery; second, the conclusion that presbytery should not appear in the paternalistic guise of forcing Alinsky on the poverty communities. The striking of the specific reference to the IAF served both of these purposes. It assured a unanimous report, and it placed the decision squarely before the indigenous population of the poverty areas. It is evident, however, that most of the moderates expected the report to lead to Alinsky's invitation.

The simplest position on the spectrum was stated by Don Buteyn, the man who led the loyal or moderate opposition to the CORAR proposal. His feeling was this: the report had no effect on whether or not Alinsky would come because he never would have come anyway and the community would never have asked him. Astute and informed members of the opposition received the committee report favorably since they generally viewed the modification as a backing away from the April 12 decision to invite Alinsky. More significant, though, was the feeling that although the committee did announce Alinsky as the prime candidate, the report would have the effect of making it extremely difficult to elicit the needed invitation. The report, by putting the responsibility for the invitation directly in the hands of the indigenous population, cut off the chance for CORAR to engage in preorganization. In view of the scattered and fragmented nature of the Oakland community, this single factor was expected to make it impossible for the IAF to receive an invitation. Finally, the most extreme opposition simply refused to hear the actual words of the report and believed that the decision was *not* to invite Alinsky.

During subsequent months, CORAR members on sober reappraisal tended to adopt the opinion of the informed opposition. As Sanderson put it, "There is no question that it made it tougher to organize for Alinsky." Although Sanderson agrees that the report delayed CORAR's response and confused the ghetto, he still thinks that the report was better than other possibilities insofar as it validated CORAR and represented a return to objectivity. Gertmenian does not share this appraisal: "Our feeling that we could get Alinsky under the call provision turned out to be an illusion. In retrospect, we should have done it otherwise." Illingworth agrees with this opinion: "The restrictions tie our hands. No one realized how difficult it would be to undergird the report." Most members of the bipartisan committee feel similarly. When the report was written, a probable majority of committee members were favorable to the idea of working with Alinsky, and all the members felt that the report left that possibility open. As one of the more conservative members put it, "We all thought Alinsky would be asked, but instead the report killed pre-organization and therefore the entire plan to get the IAF." Another member states: "The report was a defeat for CORAR, but we didn't know it. We said it to the wind. We drew a circle that kept him out."

Developments Immediately Following June 7. Although June 7 marked the end of intense concern in most Presbyterian quarters, it did not, by any means, spell the end of CORAR's efforts. Under the report, it was CORAR's job to submit to the General Council documents containing (1) criteria for determining the validity of requests for the $200,000 and (2) procedures for raising the needed funds. In a memorandum entitled "Procedures by which the people indigenous to the poverty community areas shall themselves decide democratically what, if any, community organization services are desired," CORAR suggested that a number of procedures are valid, including petitions, elections, and the calling of a congress. The basic criterion for allocation of the funds is whether the request is "representative" of that community. In making this determination, attention must be paid to information concerning general conditions in the area and attitudes of organizations, churches, and leaders. A second CORAR memorandum entitled "Fund-raising plan for financial support of mass community organization services" was submitted to the General Council. The campaign was to focus on voluntary contributions from various sources, and procedures were described for making contact with potential sources and seeking to elicit donations.

Of course, even in the aftermath of June 7, CORAR remained convinced that Alinsky should be invited. Thus, interested eyes were turned to the developments within the ghettos. Would there be sufficient preorganization to muster a call for Alinsky? Would another community organization build a strong enough base to qualify on its own for the funds? Or would the entire plan die a slow death of inaction? It soon became very apparent that there would be grave problems in administering the plan. First of all, several small organizations appeared at CORAR's door requesting the funds, and they were turned away. Although the refusal to grant them funds was justified, since the groups were not representative, some Negroes interpreted the action to mean the church had been insincere—the money was promised but not given. Second, organizational efforts in Oakland ran up against the extremely knotty problem of "fragmentation" of the poverty community. Oakland's three Negro ghettos are geographically and attitudinally so split that organization is very difficult. In addition, the threat of Alinsky had the effect of eliciting concessions from Oakland authorities and giving the definite impression that things were getting better without Alinsky.

This is not to indicate, however, that community organization has remained entirely nonexistent in the Bay Area. Actually the Mission District of San Francisco has developed quite an impressive organization, and even Oakland has come up with several game efforts (EMCOR and BUMP among others). A third and somewhat different problem is the discouragement that has set in both within the church and among those ghetto leaders who know of the presbytery action. The general feeling is that too much time has passed, and now nothing can be done. Sanderson questions this interpretation by pointing to the gap between initial stages and actual take-off of community organization in the other Alinsky-organized cities. Nevertheless, a growing sense of frustration is noticeable. A final problem, perhaps the most knotty of all, is the rise of Black Power. In the spring of 1966, the Negro community was probably in a temper favorable to asking Alinsky. The principal objections would have come from the middle-class Negro leaders who would have been threatened by the new organization. Now, however, the strongest objections to working with Alinsky are coming from the radicals rather than the conservatives, and they have one basic contention: "Alinsky's a white man. We won't work with him."

For a number of reasons, one of which may very well be respect for Black Power, Alinsky has recently indicated that he is pulling out of actual community organization and going into training. Thus, an earlier proposal to establish a training institute under Alinsky in the Bay Area has come forward again for consideration. At the moment, the hopes of the CORAR leaders and other pro-Alinsky thinkers focus on getting Alinsky to set up such an institute on his own funds and then having his Negro students undertake action projects in community organization that would qualify for the promised $200,000. Presently, opinion runs over an enormous spectrum from utter disillusionment to high hopes.

Meanwhile, among the Presbyterian opposition to Alinsky, some interesting developments have taken place. After June 7, as might have been expected, interest began to wane on the topic of Alinsky and community organization. Thus, for example, membership in the Ad Hoc Appeals Committee dropped to a small fraction of what it was in early 1966. The general feeling among conservative Presbyterians seems to have been that the June 7 action effectively killed the idea of hiring Alinsky. Recently, however, as talk of Alinsky's training institute began to be heard, the conservatives have again begun to feel anxious and angry. The fear is that CORAR will bring Alinsky "in the back door" and reopen the controversy.

Alas, the conclusion of our chronology is in reality a nonconclusion. The situation seems to be as much in flux now as it has ever been. To unravel some of the complexities of the controversy, the next chapter will turn to a more analytical interpretation of the dynamics at work.

POSTSCRIPT

The foregoing analysis of "The Presbytery Decision" is confined essentially to the period between April 12 and June 7, 1966. Since the events recounted here, a period of two years has elapsed. During this time and subsequent to our data-gathering phase, which was during the summer of 1967, it now appears possible in the summer of 1968 to discern some latent functions and unrecognized consequences.

Most important for long-range considerations is the fact that the events of spring, 1966, have served to legitimize, stimulate, and encourage support for community organization. The most tangible evidence of this process of legitimization is seen in the "Report of the Standing Committee on Religion and Race," which was approved and adopted by the Synod of the Golden Gate on June 8, 1968. It listed ten goals, three of which have a direct bearing on community organization:

1. Substantially increase its [the Department of Church and Race] financial and human resources to support existing and emerging organizations of poverty and ethnic groups.
2. Allocate significant funds to train leaders in the methods of organizing the powerless, and in combating white racism.
3. Initiate and coordinate a plan in consultation with particular churches whereby these churches will become more in communication with and in direct support of specific community organization projects.

With increasing nationwide and local concern for poverty issues, symbolized by the spring, 1968, Poor People's March on Washington, D.C., and with attention turning to employment and housing conditions in the ghetto, the legitimation of community organization as a viable means for church action is a significant step that should bear important consequences.

Meanwhile, a number of Bay Area ventures in community organization have profited directly or indirectly from CORAR's efforts. In addition to groups previously mentioned, they include: Western Addition Community Organization (WACO), which has succeeded in blocking redevelopment plans in 1967 and in 1968; West Oakland Planning Commission, which campaigned successfully against the Model Cities Program in Oakland in spring, 1968; Tropicania Hillside Organization for Unity in East San Jose (THOU); and the Mission District Coalition.

3

The Politics of Non-Decision:
Analysis of Response

Our Introduction depicted a fundamental split within the Christian community concerning the church's role and purpose. CORAR's proposal to support Alinsky brought this latent dualism sharply to the surface.

From the potpourri of events and opinions, we now seek a conceptual model to shed light on what transpired at the presbytery level. Our focus here is upon the presbytery as a decision-making body and the adequacy of its tools for dealing with intense conflict. We propose to hang our analysis on the following pegs: substantive and structural dualism, polarization, the politics of non-decision, and the ambiguity of the results.

Substantive and Structural Dualism

We have contended that a basic dualism pervades the Christian enterprise. This dualism has been described as Worldly Christianity versus Churchly Christianity, comfort versus challenge, maintenance versus mission, and preservation versus prophecy. In addition to the substantive dualism there is also a parallel *structural dualism*.

What do we mean when we speak of the San Francisco Presbytery as a decision-making body? The Presbyterian Church, as is well known, has its own type of federated government. The structures of the church at large, both national and regional, have a certain amount of independent decision-making authority. Nevertheless, the local Presbyterian congregation remains a locus of important decision-making power and retains a certain monetary veto over bureaucratic activities. This "self-government," on the other hand, is not so thoroughgoing as in the case of congregational churches.

The "bureaucracy" of the Presbyterian Church exists at three main levels. First, there are the three national boards: the Commission on Ecumenical Mission and Relations, the Board of Christian Education, and the Board of National Missions. National policy, as developed by the national boards, is acted upon in the annual General Assembly. Second, there are the regional (or synod) agencies. The third organizational level is the presbytery. Preliminary discussion and decision-making is carried out through committees composed of pastors and lay delegates. These committees rely on staff officers for leadership in the formulation of programs, but they must finally look to the presbytery for approval of their programs. Presbytery comprises ordained clergymen plus elected lay delegates from member congregations.

What, then, do the events of 1966 tell us about the composition and attitudes of the Presbyterian bureaucracy? To put it another way, where does the church bureaucracy stand in relation to the two poles of contemporary Christianity? In the first place, it is well known that some of the church's most astute social activists and political tacticians are on the Board of National Missions. They have sought to assist local leaders to move into secular involvement. Hence, the Board has been singled out as the champion of the advocates of Worldly Christianity. Consequently it has come in for ever-increasing attacks by more conservative elements in the church.

The internal bureaucratic struggles of the national church are beyond the scope of this study. Our research, however, has unearthed some interesting data concerning similar developments within the Bay Area. In the late fifties and early sixties, when the call for greater church involvement in the secular world began to be intensified, the activists in San Francisco Presbytery appraised the situation and decided to implement their programs by assuming a larger role in positions of leadership. Gradually, through the ensuing years, the new leaders consolidated their hold on the bureaucracy by appointing liberal majorities to presbytery committees and to permanent staff positions. By the time of the Alinsky dispute, the activist position had become institutionalized.

Control over CORAR, as we have seen, was particularly significant. When CORAR was reactivated in early 1966, the liberal majority had a clear agenda which allowed full-time concentration on the Alinsky proposal. This institutional base was to give the pro-Alinsky forces a significant tactical advantage over their unorganized opposition.

The bureaucratic changing of the guard, however, does not necessarily reflect the overall position of the laity regarding the priority of the challenge-mission-prophecy agenda. There can be little doubt, for example, that the bulk of monetary support for presbytery action was coming from parishes whose clergy and laity had substantial reservations concerning the worldly involvement programs of the new leadership. Thus, in some ways, the Presbyterian Church of early 1966 was similar to the Republican Party: it had within its ranks a sharp spilt between conservatives and liberals. A major difference, however, was that in the Presbyterian Church the liberals held the command posts. Another factor worth noting is that the liberals had enhanced their voting power in presbytery through occupying various nonparish positions, which did not represent any particular group of laity. Thus, the liberal majority included many staff men, mission pastors, and others. In short, at the time of the Alinsky proposal, the liberals' tactical position had become independent of lay support, and they were in a position to lead the laity into action which the laity itself might not have initiated.

Essentially, then, the structural situation that existed in

early 1966 involved two powerful competing elites. The conservative elite consisted of a numerical minority of conservative clergy and perhaps a majority of laymen. Formerly in power, this group now found itself displaced. Thus at the time of the CORAR proposal the conservatives were ill prepared and poorly organized. Opposing the conservative elite was the new elite of activists. This group was better organized than the conservatives.

By early 1966, the advocates of Worldly Christianity had consolidated a position of influence that allowed them to initiate action on issues involving a degree of social involvement which would have been prohibitive under the previously prevailing Presbyterian ethos. Thus, the issue facing the liberal elite was how far to press their advantage. What could the church handle at that particular time in its history? The racial crisis brought this matter to a point of urgency in 1965 and 1966. Our data indicate that this issue was decided upon by Bay Area leaders acting on their own initiative. The coalition of Sanderson and the "caucus group" determined that the time was ripe to confront the church with the necessity of decision-making on community organization. There can be little doubt that this decision was one of the most advanced and precarious efforts to move the church into community action up to that time.

This analysis of the structural dualism within the Presbyterian Church raises some important questions for further study. First, there is the empirical question concerning the degree to which the "institutionalized liberal position" diverges from the attitudes of the mass of Presbyterian laity. To what extent has the constituency come along with their leaders? Our tentative hypothesis was that a substantial gap had opened between the leaders and the masses. If this proved true, significant theoretical questions would be implied. For example, how is genuine institutional change best achieved? By confrontation? By fiat? By accretion? By revolution? By consensus? Again, what structural recourse remained open for the opponents of the trend? Finally, what was the nature of the relationship between the leaders and the laity?

THE DUALISM IS SURFACED AND SHARPENED: POLARIZATION

In addition to our original hypothesis concerning the dualism within the Presbyterian Church, we hypothesized that the proposal to affiliate with Alinsky would bring the latent split to the surface with explosive force. Although there was much impressionistic evidence that the writings of the new breed of worldly theologians and ethicists were having some effect on Presbyterians, it seemed clear that the church could hardly be described as a radical action corps. Saul Alinsky himself was controversial enough to provoke heated debate, but several other factors exacerbated the conflict. These factors originated primarily in CORAR's tactics for presenting the proposal. An appraisal of these tactics raises at least three independent questions: (1) What decisions were made? (2) Why were these decisions made? (3) What was the effect of these decisions? On each of these questions, the data are confusing and contradictory. There is agreement on one point, however: the most controversial matter concerns the amount of advance notice and information given by CORAR to the Bay Area presbyters. Most of the delegates received the "call" for the emergency meeting on the Friday before Palm Sunday. Some educational efforts were made before the April 12 meeting, such as distributing mimeographed materials and conducting breakfast meetings. Nevertheless, the general feeling among both proponents and opponents, at least in retrospect, was that the advance preparation had been inadequate.

The first question, then, is whether a decision was made to suppress information and spring the matter on an unprepared presbytery. At least a few leaders may have been motivated by such a hope. After all, there were reasonable grounds for assuming that if the presbytery had been fully informed about the proposed action, the opponents would have organized to defeat the motion. Thus, some of the pro-Alinsky forces may have felt that the only way to ensure passage was to mobilize the proponents and keep the opponents in the dark. And, in fact, some of the people who were involved in the pre-April 12 deliberations recall that this matter was discussed. There is, on the other hand, much contrary evidence to negate this theory. In the first place, the men most deeply involved in the planning categorically deny any such intention. Of course, it might be held to be in their interest to conceal the fact even if it were true, but before we jump to any conclusions, let us examine the situation. Perhaps the most significant piece of evidence that contradicts the "suppression of information" hypothesis is that the proposal was presented in full to San Jose Presbytery on March 26 after more than a month's notice. This seems inconsistent with a conspiracy to suppress notice. In fact, our evidence is that the pro-Alinsky forces went away from the San Jose meeting convinced that they would have to *increase* their efforts to prepare the San Francisco delegates. And, of course, it is clearly established that CORAR mailed an information packet to all the San Francisco delegates. In short, although there is some reason to believe that at least a few individuals wanted to "sock it to 'em," the evidence by and large supports the conclusion that there was no con-spiracy to suppress information.

If this is true, then why wasn't more advance notice given? Here it is possible to isolate several factors. First, there is the testimony of many leaders that CORAR mistakenly as-sumed that the presbytery was already prepared to handle the issue. The following quotation from a later CORAR document may be taken as an illustration: "In view of this perspective (past involvement) and heritage of teaching and proclamation, CORAR assumed that a firm basis for commitment to action has been established." This assumption was presumably based on the earlier confrontation with Proposition 14 and with the extensive coverage of Alinsky in the national media. That such an assumption was naïve is certainly proven by the subsequent uproar. Furthermore, it seems particularly ingenuous in view of the decisive victory of Proposition 14.

Another factor in the lack of preparation and in the timing generally is the simple fact of impatience. For one thing, the liberals admit that they had grown increasingly tired of the church's inaction and wanted to force the issue. This was enhanced by the general infatuation with Alinsky. More significantly, and this can hardly be denied, many of the pro-CORAR forces were genuinely afraid that Oakland would explode into a full-scale riot in the summer of 1966 unless the Negroes felt that help was on the way. There is some controversy about the position of the most knowledgeable leaders on this matter: apparently some people, including Alinsky himself, had predicted that Oakland would not riot because of the fragmented character of the Negro population. Thus, it may be that a few of the more radical leaders used the riot threat as a tactical gambit. Nevertheless, it is certain that most of the members of CORAR were genuinely afraid of the riot prediction and felt an extreme sense of urgency. In short, there are many reasons why the timing and preparation was as it was, and no clear reason to assume that the plan was to railroad the proposal through an unprepared presbytery.

The final question is whether the timing and lack of preparation was a tactical mistake. Here a complicating factor appears. The failure of CORAR to make contact with the laity opened the way for the *Oakland Tribune* to reach a large number of unprepared Presbyterians. It has been hypothesized that individuals who knew nothing of Alinsky were thrown into a "blue panic" by this article. Thus, in addition to the anger at CORAR's supposed bad faith, the "monster myth" about Alinsky was given a head start. We must, however, forgo for the moment the temptation to jump to the easy conclusion and berate CORAR for its bad faith or mistaken judgment. Sanderson, for example, although he is willing to admit that the assumption of Presbyterian readiness for the Alinsky issue was mistaken, is not so certain that the lack of advance preparation was bad. His theory, supported by reputable students of social change, is that the threat of the April 12 decision forced Presbyterians to educate themselves. We will discuss this "education through encounter" hypothesis in relation to our congregation studies later.

Viewing the matter from a slightly different perspective, however, we find good reason to conclude that the tactics, whether chosen or accidental, were not optimum for this situation. The perspective we refer to is the general substantive and structural context of the proposal earlier discussed. If our conclusions are correct, then the presbytery already suffered from a deep, latent division over the purpose of the church. It should have been apparent, therefore, that this controversial proposal to align the church with Alinsky would be a difficult pill for the more conservative Presbyterians to swallow. Thus, it should have been recognized that the presbytery was faced with extremely delicate tactical questions, and that the matter should have been handled so as to avoid any peripheral issues concerning the good faith of fellow churchmen. Thus, for example, greater efforts should have been made to indulge the opponents at the April 12 meeting. Many opposition leaders felt anger and resentment over the "rude" treatment they received when they tried to express their position on the proposal.

Finally, of course, an appraisal of the tactics raises questions that cannot be answered now and perhaps can never be fully answered. Was the overall Alinsky experience good or bad for the Presbyterian Church? Would the experience have been equally good or bad had it been done differently? For those who feel that the church profited from the encounter, there is the risk that advance preparation might have eventuated in the defeat of the proposal on April 12 without any major stir in the church at all.

The point to underscore is that polarization definitely occurred. From April 12 to April 26, the presbytery was in extreme turmoil. The two factions faced each other with great

hostility. Rumors flew thick and fast. Unjustifiable charges
were in the air. Threats and recriminations were rampant. The
presbytery was polarized.

THE POLITICS OF NON-DECISION

At this point, we enter the arena of our own interpretation.
The hypothesis we suggest is that the processes for dealing
with conflict collapsed under the Alinsky issue and that the
action taken on June 7 was in actuality a non-decision which
relieved presbytery of the need to confront the substantive
issue and work out a genuine resolution. As we have mentioned, the June 7 decision was interpreted by both the pro-
Alinsky and anti-Alinsky factions as a victory. CORAR felt
that the vote validated the April 12 action. After all, the report
called for community organization and stated that Alinsky
and the IAF were in a class by themselves. Thus, as soon as
the ghettos issued a representative call for Alinsky, the $200,-
000 would be used as planned by CORAR. The anti-Alinsky
group, on the other hand, interpreted the decision as a backing away from the April 12 action. For most of the opposition,
it sufficed that the specific reference to Alinsky was stricken.
Without noticing the commendation of Alinsky in the committee report, they breathed a sigh of relief and assumed that
the matter was dead. Only a few canny opponents saw, as
CORAR was soon to realize, that the report had a hidden
feature that would probably produce a *de facto* defeat for
CORAR.

Let us turn our attention to the June 7 decision. As will be
recalled, the gist of the committee's recommendations was to
strike the name of Alinsky and to promise the $200,000 to
community organization ventures that were *representative* of
the ghetto. Whether Alinsky's name would be included or
excluded had been the decisive question. The decision to ex-
clude was reached for two reasons: (1) in order to avoid the
challenge of "paternalism" which might have ensued if the

presbytery tried to push Alinsky on the ghettos and (2) in order to reach a compromise that would be acceptable to both factions and restore amity to the presbytery. Note that with only *one* possible exception, the entire bipartisan committee expected their report would allow Alinsky to receive the $200,000. Even more significant is the fact that the report *would not have been made as it was* had the liberals and moderates known that it would preclude the hiring of Alinsky. CORAR also was faced at this time with the question of whether to fight the report or try to work within its provisions. The decision reached was the latter.

Why was this a "non-decision"? The answer to this question lies in one crucial factor that had been overlooked: the Oakland ghettos that comprised the principal target were so fragmented that they would be unable to muster a "representative request" on their own. The obviousness of this fact is evident from the speed with which it was recognized by all interested parties: the recognition appeared almost as soon as CORAR attempted implementation. It seems strange that this fact was missed by disciples of Alinsky, whose first tenet is to "know your community."

Why was the fact of Oakland's fragmentation overlooked? The only apparent answer is that the moderate and liberal backers were blinded by their fear of reopening the conflict. To be sure, one reason for striking the reference to Alinsky was to avoid paternalism and allow the ghettos to decide for themselves. Moreover, blinded by their desire for peace, the presbytery threw the decision back to the ghettos, which were unprepared to make it. The upshot was a "non-decision," which gave everyone a feeling of victory and left the offer of funds to die of inaction.

The thrust of this analysis, therefore, calls into question the myth of the "divine authorship" of Presbyterian bipartisan committee reports. The sole opinion which unified a vast majority of our informants—that the committee report was a masterpiece and the June 7 meeting a noble achievement—

seems to evaporate in irony. The widely held conclusion that
Presbyterian polity proved itself able to handle the challenge
appears untenable. The June 7 action turns out to be pure
conflict resolution and substantive non-decision, a purchase of
peace by retreating from the battle.

In this perspective James Coleman has presented an analysis of the dynamics of conflict that sheds light on the presbytery struggle. According to Coleman, conflict situations have
an inherent tendency to shift their focus from substantive
issues to personalities. Thus, disagreement over even a minor
matter can provide a context in which hidden anger comes to
the surface. In this process, the original cause of disagreement
is often forgotten, and arguments become increasingly *ad
hominem*. Finally, a stage is reached in which those parties involved in the controversy become so enraged that they un-
leash a full-scale attack on their opponents' character. At this
point, the conflict becomes functionally autonomous and the
original issue is totally obscured. Coleman's thesis is that
"proper" handling of conflict avoids this development and
succeeds in keeping the discussion focused on the actual substantive issues involved.

To some extent, Coleman's analysis is not exactly in point.
The chief difficulty is that the question of Alinsky's personality
lies somewhere in the gray area between substantive issues
and *ad hominem* argument. Although the *Oakland Tribune*
may be largely to blame, there can be little doubt that the
explosion beginning on April 12 got out of hand. Personalities
became so totally involved that the actual issues were nearly
lost sight of. So intense was this conflict that leaders were
blinded to the substantive realities and settled for a peace at
any cost.

This analysis of the dynamics of the conflict provides a
significant commentary on the present state of churches in
general. It is widely recognized that the church is inadequately
equipped to handle conflict. One of the great shibboleths of
Christian ministry has traditionally been "reconciliation." Al-

though reconciliation presumably presupposes prior conflict, the church has, in fact, taken great pains to avoid all outbreaks of conflict within its ranks and to maintain a state of peaceful coexistence among its members. Georg Simmel, the pioneer German sociologist, has explained the situation in the following way. Conflict, he says, is an unavoidable aspect of the life of institutions which deal with scarce values. The church, however, has been able to avoid conflict and survive because its commodity is the grace of God, and that by definition is an abundant commodity. Thus conflict has not been a necessary feature of church life. The obvious fact, however, is that worldly involvement has begun to push the church into the realm of scarce values. This has had the effect of precipitating the church into conflict situations for which it is unprepared.

The upshot of this discussion is that the church must develop expertise in handling conflict if it is to continue in its worldly involvement. The events within San Francisco Presbytery in the first half of 1966 bear this out. This inability to cope with intense conflict will be a hypothesis to examine in the ensuing congregational studies.

THE AMBIGUITY OF THE RESULTS

Our analysis has emphasized the substantive and structural dualism within the Presbyterian Church, the polarization that occurred when the Alinsky issue surfaced and exacerbated the already existing split, and the inadequacy of the church's tools for conflict resolution. In addition, we have seen that a number of miscalculations were made in handling the issue, namely, inadequate preparation, inadequate communication, recrimination from both sides, failure to ensure that the motion could be tabled, failure to take Oakland's uniqueness seriously, and others. In such a situation, it is not at all surprising that the effects of the controversy are somewhat ambiguous.

First, what were the results for the Bay Area's Negro communities? The non-decision of June 7 threw the decision back onto the shoulders of the ghettos. Since they have not generated a representative request for the funds, no direct action has been taken. Thus, two years later, the matter stands much as it was left on June 7, 1966. This situation, of course, cannot be laid entirely at the doorstep of the church. At least two intervening variables made the Presbyterian offer more problematic. First came the rise of Black Power and with it a heightened resistance to any form of alignment with either white churches or white community organizers. Secondly, the federal government began to respond to the racial problem by funding programs similar to that proposed by the church.

There has been some speculation, however, concerning certain indirect benefits to the Negro communities. Even if the process did not result in hiring Alinsky, the threat may have given rise to increased awareness and action through other channels. Nearly all our informants, for example, felt that the threat produced increased efforts by existing groups and also gave rise to some new programs for dealing with the racial situation. We shall refer to the latter as "spin-off programs." One significant hypothesis for further study, then, is that the debate succeeded in moving at least some individuals off the dime and into a variety of programs for dealing with racial and poverty problems.

There has been some speculation, in addition, concerning a possible change in the attitudes of the Negro community toward the Presbyterian Church. Persons identified with CORAR's proposal feel that many Negroes have come to understand that the church is trying to help and can be viewed as an ally. This contention could be tested only by a broad survey of Bay Area Negro communities, but there are several reasons to doubt the speculation. In the first place, although the original action may have raised some Negro hopes, the subsequent failure to disburse the funds, coupled with the refusal of several requests, may have created a feeling of disillusionment among even those who had been favorably impressed. CORAR's opponents, for example, feel that the experience has left the Negroes with the feeling that the Presbyterian Church is a phony, which promises but fails to produce action. The more telling consideration, however, is the simple fact that, apart from a few leaders, very few Bay Area Negroes know anything at all about what went on within the church. Thus, it appears that the presbytery action has had little effect on either the attitudes or the actual situation of the Bay Area Negroes.

In short, the only arena where substantial effects may have occurred is within the Presbyterian Church. The proposal for social action seems to have turned in on the church and reduced itself to an internal squabble. The question that remains, therefore, concerns the internal effects of the controversy. Here also we meet with ambiguity. The effects, of course, cannot be analyzed with finality until we have seen what transpired within local congregations in the Bay Area. At this stage, we can only make certain suggestions in the form of hypotheses for further study.

First, in our interviews with presbytery leaders, much was said about the educational effects of the controversy. Presbytery staff executives, for example, felt that the period from April to June, 1966, represents the most intensive educational experience ever for San Francisco Presbyterians. As we have seen, substantive education on race and poverty problems was attempted through at least three channels: the bipartisan committee, the CORAR publications and area meetings, and the activities of the Ad Hoc Appeals Committee. Furthermore, the high degree of interest generated may have increased the effectiveness of the formal educational efforts. Thus, one hypothesis for further testing is that the controversy gave rise to considerable education on the questions of racial problems and modes of response.

Another frequently mentioned effect of the controversy concerns an allegedly increased ability and willingness to deal with conflict situations. Although some of the opposition felt that there had been a destructive division and increase of hostility, many of our informants referred to an increased openness to conflict situations and honesty in the expression of controversial viewpoints. They feel that the presbytery has "grown up" and that the conservatives are being taught the lesson of the unavoidability of conflict. A second hypothesis, therefore, is that the local congregations will reveal an increased tolerance for and ability to cope with conflict as a consequence of the 1966 debate.

A third area for further study concerns the effect of the controversy on relations among Bay Area Presbyterians. Some of our informants suggested that there had been an increase of hostility, a breakdown of communication, and a general alienation of Presbyterians from their church. Others, however, felt that the experience had been highly beneficial for church members. They argue that there has been no substantial loss of membership or pledges and that the experience with the Alinsky proposal has, in fact, made the church a more tightly knit institution. In their opinion, the June 7 meeting represented a genuine resolution of the conflict and an advance toward a more effective coalition of differing factions. Answers to these questions will be sought in subsequent chapters.

Part Two of our study presents case studies of four varying congregational responses. With the perspectives thus far developed regarding substantive and structural dualism, decision-making processes, educational potential, willingness to confront conflict, and the consequences of conflict, we are now ready to explore the impact of the Alinsky controversy at the local parish level.

PART TWO
THE IMPACT ON LOCAL CONGREGATIONS

4
Christ Church

Christ Church's response to the Alinsky proposal was one of strong support. With its reputation for being liberal and socially alert, this atypical suburban congregation should provide valuable clues for understanding the church's attempt to be "involved in the world."

Until 1950 Christ Church, in Jefferson, resembled many other small-town, Protestant churches. It was "the" established neighborhood church. During the fifties, two events radically transformed Christ Church. In 1952 the quiet, semi-agricultural town of Jefferson, famous for its white table wines, suddenly became a humming scientific community concerned with the technology of atomic energy. The next decade saw an influx of technical competence: 450 persons with Ph.D.'s, nearly 2,000 persons with lesser advanced degrees, and over 3,500 technical and mechanical specialists. By 1964 the estimated employment in the town was 15,400 persons, over half of whom were directly employed in jobs connected with atomic research and development.

Another decisive event for Christ Church was the calling of Rev. Robert Sharp as pastor in 1957. A dynamic and sensitive leader, Mr. Sharp came into the life of the congregation at a moment of flux and uncertainty. By restructuring the church and by emphasizing lay leadership, he helped the congregation redefine its purpose and plot its new course into the future.

Of course, not all the lines of continuity with the past were severed. Yet little doubt remains that the congregation has moved rapidly away from the small-town, neighborhood church that characterized the 1950's.

CHARACTERISTICS OF THE CONGREGATION

Socioeconomic Characteristics. Occupationally speaking, Christ Church is unique. Its 1,200 members, nearly half of whom attend Sunday worship services, are largely upper middle class with an average yearly income of $10,000. Because of the scientific nature of the town's principal industry, the educational level is very high. In political affiliation, the church is divided evenly. Church staff consists of three pastors and one secretary.

Theological Orientation. When the members of Christ Church were asked to define the *nature* of the church, the theme they used repeatedly was "agent of social change." Moreover, the character of this change was depicted as man's social and environmental well-being. The following is a typical statement: "The nature of the church is to seek to change men and society. It is to improve mankind and his condition on this earth." Only two persons described the nature of the church in terms of its relationship with God. The major thrust was definitely in the direction of the church's relationship to man in his social context.

This same attitude is reflected in the way members defined the purpose of their congregation as "mission to the larger community." "Our goal is to bring health and wholeness to the life of man." "We should be working to help people experience what it means to be fully human." "Our purpose is to become an instrument for social progress." Community service is seen as taking two directions. The first involves supplying leadership for important civic positions. (In 1966 three of the five members on the Jefferson Municipal Council were active church members.) The second direction is to develop programs designed to meet community problems.

Our informants all affirmed that the church should definitely take stands on sociopolitical issues. The only qualifying remark was that "taking a stand ought not to shut off dissenting voices, that is, a stand should not cut off communication." A strong feeling persisted that taking a stand and open, free debate go hand in hand, that education and involvement go together; moreover, it was felt that churches should teach and encourage members to be involved in social problems. They believe the church should make every effort: (1) to help its members be keenly aware of the facts; (2) to sensitize the members to the human needs involved; (3) to provide a context for decision-making on issues; and (4) to enable them to enact their decision. In responding to community problems such as race and poverty, our informants saw both individual and corporate response as legitimate and necessary.

An important dimension of Christ Church's theological orientation is the belief that the vitality of the church depends upon the quality of its laymen. One of the principal means for developing well-informed lay leaders is the adult education program which has two key features. The first is book clubs or groups that "seek, through discussion of books and encounter with one another, to better understand themselves and the world in the light of the Christian faith." The second feature is education classes held on Sunday mornings. Set up in six- or twelve-week cycles, these classes focus chiefly on relating Christian faith to current social problems. Courses taught during 1966 included "Missionary—Modern Style," "The Christian Citizen," "Christians in Families," and "Christianity and Children."

The organizational life of Christ Church is also a means for developing articulate laymen. Mr. Sharp and three of the laymen, all of whom were well acquainted with organizational theory, designed a system for developing the leadership potential of Christ Church members. In commenting on this organization structure, Mr. Sharp said: "In order for the church to be effective I think you have to have a church structure that will give power to lay leaders by allowing them to take a more aggressive role in the session and by encouraging people to take differing viewpoints. Being on session shouldn't amount to playing follow the leader. I think each person has leadership possibilities, but they need to be given the chance to realize those possibilities. In our organizational structure we give a lay leader an area of concern and allow him to be responsible for it. Our lay leaders and clergy are co-workers. Now I'm not saying that the pastor should just be a resource person, for he needs to be a strong leader too. However, he should encourage and allow others to take strong stands too."

Specific action programs also reflect the theological orientation of Christ Church. Their focus is on the church's attempt to involve itself in concrete social situations. The first major attempt came in 1964 when the session decided to take a definite stand against Proposition 14, that is, against the repeal of the state's open housing legislation. A second line of action was exposure to the lives of people directly affected by problems of racial prejudice and poverty. For a group of twenty to thirty persons, this involvement included a membership exchange program with an Oakland inner-city church. Moreover, a third minister was added to the staff to direct the Division of Mission and Youth. This new position was created for the expressed purpose of enabling the church to realize more fully its "ministry to the world."

In short, since 1964 the church has been deliberately moving toward a serious involvement with sociopolitical issues. It is not an overstatement to say that all the major dimensions of the church's life—pastoral ministry, education program, stewardship, etc.—have been geared around this attempt to redefine the purpose of the church to make life more human by working for change in the political structures.

Pastoral Leadership. Mr. Sharp is a dynamic world-oriented pastor who sees his role at Christ Church as one of enabling the congregation to become a community of sensitive Christians who take seriously their mission to the world. During the past ten years the congregation in redefining its purpose has gradually formulated a new style of life. If the members had been unreceptive to new questions and new directions, however, Mr. Sharp's hopes for a socially conscious church would certainly have been dubious. The reorganization of the congregation, the creation of a strong adult education program, and the active involvement of the church in sociopolitical affairs indicate that the search for a new identity at Christ Church has been a corporate venture.

Although an able administrator, a fine teacher, and an excellent preacher, the members prefer to characterize Mr. Sharp as a "tremendous pastor." His greatest strength is his ability to relate to people. Some parishioners may feel their pastor is sometimes mistaken in his opinions, but no one thinks he is unfair or "has an ax to grind." He is described as a man "who is able to create an atmosphere of trust because he doesn't ride a white charger." His leadership has deepened the personal relationships within the congregation and moved the congregation toward a greater commitment to social action.

Past Experience. Christ Church was deeply involved in the Proposition 14 controversy. Several members had been active in the issue of open housing years before Proposition 14 appeared on the ballot. The pastor and several lay leaders helped to organize a fair housing group for open housing covenants. When petitions to place 14 on the ballot were circulated, Mr. Sharp and others in this group urged the members not to sign them. Once the issue was on the ballot, the open housing committee organized a "Vote No on Proposition 14" campaign. This group was very active both in the church and community. They requested and were granted permission to speak to various groups in the church. The session sent out a letter urging the congregation to vote no. Strong support was expressed for open housing. Naturally, those who worked to defeat Proposition 14 were deeply disappointed when the proposition passed by an overwhelming majority of 2 to 1. Looking back at the controversy, Mr. Sharp comments: "If I could do it again, I would have public meetings where both sides could express their views. Then I would urge the session to send out a letter which would explain its stand, but would not hinder anyone in taking an opposite view."

Even before the conflict over Proposition 14 had subsided, Christ Church was plunged into another controversy—this time over the proposal to build a new sanctuary and education facilities. The first question was whether to move to another location. After careful study of the church's growth pattern, the community's needs, and the congregation's purpose, the committee recommended that the congregation remain at its site. Members accepted this decision which, in effect, meant staying near the central business district rather than moving to the countryside.

Next came the question of financing the new facilities. As one man put it: "To some the cost was staggering." The session and the building committee recommended that the congregation build only part of the proposed facilities. They felt that this plan would ease the financial burden. The congregation, however, voted to undertake the entire building program and to support it financially.

Although strong differences of opinion were expressed over various aspects of the building program, the controversy moved in an orderly way to a resolution that was unanimously acceptable. One reason this controversy took such a creative course is that the leadership anticipated conflict and established organizational structures and procedures to deal with it.

Thus in the two years prior to the Alinsky issue the congregation had experienced two major controversies. In Proposition 14 the church collided head on with the racial issue. As a result of the conflict, a few members left the church, and even today there continues to be some grumbling about the vigorous stand taken by the pastor and session. However, the next controversy produced different consequences. June 5, 1965, marked the dedication of the new additions to the church and thereby symbolized the successful consummation of the building program controversy.

Structural Elements. In recent years an increasing number of technically competent younger persons have moved into leadership positions. In the early 1960's, four younger men were elected to session. That election marked the beginning of a displacement of the older leadership, and by 1964 that process was completed. Despite the congregation's split over Proposition 14, most of the members supported the direction in which these new leaders were moving the church. Some of the older leaders voiced occasional disapproval, but they did not challenge the newer leadership elite.

The new leaders maintained excellent communications among themselves. Almost all of them have been actively involved in the book discussion groups, and the notion of growth through "encountering one another" has carried over into their work on session. This leadership elite has also sought to maintain good communication with the rest of the congregation. In addition to being well informed about their local situation, these leaders make a real effort to keep up to date on presbytery activities. Mr. Sharp is actively involved in presbytery and thus is an excellent source of information.

An annual leadership retreat is held at the beginning of each year to evaluate how well the church is meeting its objectives. This retreat, notes the pastor, provides "an opportunity for asking what we are doing and where we are 'goofing up.' There are no inspirational talks, no outside speakers, and no fancy worship services." In January, 1966, the primary topic of discussion was how to deal with social controversy within the church. After the shake-up following Proposition 14, some of the leaders felt a need for guidelines that would steer the church in a "more creative direction." At the retreat, three months before the Alinsky controversy, strategy was outlined for handling controversial issues. Included in this outline were such things as: interpretative sermons, general congregational meetings for the purpose of supplying information and encouraging discussion, making printed materials available that explained the position of both sides, etc. It was also decided that it would probably be better not to call for a congregational vote on such matters and instead make a maximum effort to educate rather than persuade. The objective behind this strategy was to create a context in which the congregation could encounter a controversial issue without being polarized to such a degree that neither substantive education nor direct action could take place.

Hence, when the Alinsky controversy erupted, it came to a church that had: (1) a definite commitment to concrete political action; (2) a leadership sensitive to the dynamics of serious controversy; (3) a membership that had recently lived through two major controversies; and (4) an organizational structure that had produced a relatively large number of active and well-informed laymen, many of whom possessed a keen sense of social justice.

DYNAMICS OF DECISION-MAKING

The announcement of CORAR's intention to ask the San Francisco Presbytery to support Alinsky crossed Mr. Sharp's desk during Holy Week. He informed the delegates to presbytery of the issue to be discussed at the special meeting and advised them to read something about Alinsky. Although Mr. Sharp advised them to expect a battle, they did not anticipate a major controversy. All seven delegates voted for the proposal at the April 12 presbytery meeting.

On April 14 the entire membership learned about presbytery's action through the front page of the *Oakland Tribune*.

"Deeply disturbed" most accurately characterizes the response of some parishioners. Two members, who were the most upset, angrily protested to the delegates. The pastor received three irate phone calls. Although the majority of the congregation was not disturbed, many were confused about the problem, what the rationale of the proposal was, and what the presbytery vote really meant.

Many discussions about Alinsky followed, with the emotional high-water mark being reached on the first Sunday after the vote. The congregation came to worship that morning deeply alarmed by what it had read in the newspaper. After Mr. Sharp defined the situation, however, the congregation began to "calm down." At the service, he explained to the congregation the reason for the action and its implications. He also explained that this matter was not a local issue calling for a congregational or session vote. He did point out, however, that every effort would be made in Christ Church to discuss the issues involved, that petitions for a reconsideration of the question were being filed, and that the whole matter would come before presbytery again.

When asked to describe the congregation's knowledge of Bay Area race and poverty problems, our informants all agreed that the congregation itself was only vaguely aware of the issues. Perhaps two dozen people, most of them church leaders, were well informed about specific aspects of these problems. Except for a few persons, however, there was little awareness of community organization as a social action strategy, of Saul Alinsky and the Industrial Areas Foundation, or of the purposes and activities of CORAR. Leaders who did have some knowledge of these matters held a positive attitude toward them, as witnessed by the fact that all the delegates to presbytery and all the session members supported the Alinsky proposal.

Once the controversy began, two different groups in the church were raising two types of concerns. A small, but very vocal group of a dozen people immediately questioned the legitimacy of the church's intention to become involved in politics. One lay leader estimated that "at best they spoke for the feelings of 15 percent, perhaps 20 percent, of the 1200 members." The majority of the members were asking the question: Is this the style of social action with which we want to identify? By mid-April, after some initial discussion had taken place, a large number of the congregation could agree that the sociopolitical problems of the larger community did constitute a legitimate arena for active church involvement. By the end of April they could agree also that the problems of the Negro ghetto urgently called for some form of social action.

The major part of the April–May discussions centered on the style of Saul Alinsky's community action. Many voiced an uneasiness about his militancy and questioned whether it was appropriate for the Christian church to identify with such tactics. Although one informant claimed that "several persons moved from skepticism to acceptance," another indicated that many persons were "relieved by the presbytery's final action because they believed they could now solve the problems in Oakland without Alinsky." Still another lay leader estimated that as many as 40 percent of the people were for community organization, but opposed to Alinsky.

Once the controversy was under way the congregation looked primarily to the pastor for information. Mr. Sharp reflected this situation when he said that he "told the story (i.e., presbytery's action, Alinsky's program, etc.) at least thirty times." He kept the congregation informed by weekly announcements from the pulpit, by talking to adult education classes, and by personal discussions. Two of the delegates assisted the pastor in this task, and the session distributed CORAR's information packet, but for the most part, the pastor was the main source of reliable information.

Another source of information was a CORAR area meeting held at Christ Church and attended by over two hundred persons. Members from Christ Church at the meeting felt the man who spoke against the proposal "just tried to muddy the waters." Most opined that the meeting had very little educational benefit.

We now focus attention on the actual decision-making process at Christ Church during the Alinsky controversy. We will look at the following: (1) influential persons, (2) organization, (3) content of the decision, and (4) extent of membership involvement.

It was generally felt that the pastor was the single most influential force in shaping the decision. Certain lay leaders and the session itself were also influential. But the members regarded the pastor as the key figure. Mr. Sharp outlined his approach this way: "First, I explained to the people what the facts were. Then, I tried to interpret the action of presbytery. Lastly, I described Saul Alinsky, community organization, and the problems which existed in the ghetto. I urged people to take whatever stand they wanted, but at the same time I reminded them that presbytery had the right to act. I myself took a strong affirmative position and made this known." Mr. Sharp implemented this strategy through sermons, prayers, formal and informal discussions, and personal calls. He made a special effort to confer personally with those members who were opposed to the action taken.

Certain laymen also played an influential role in the decision-making process. Both the delegates to presbytery and the session members, all of whom favored the Alinsky proposal, made their thinking widely known. Hence not a single opposing voice was raised from the official lay leaders of the congregation. Moreover, no organized opposition emerged from the congregation. To be sure, some prominent persons voiced reservations, but they held no church offices and they did not attempt an organized protest. Most of the lay leaders were involved in attempts to explain and interpret the presbytery's action. The book club groups and the adult education classes both provided places for church leaders to inform the congregation about community organization, Alinsky, poverty issues, etc.

Most members thought that although they did not provide a rubber stamp endorsement of the leadership's position, they supported their leaders' views. When asked why they did so, most felt it was due to "the atmosphere of trust which Mr. Sharp has done so much to create." One informant said: "Rev. Mr. Sharp set a mood of confidence and trust during the controversy over Alinsky. He didn't ride a white charger. He took a strong position and encouraged others to do the same." In terms of three groups that existed at Christ Church during the controversy, Mr. Sharp's influence could be described as follows:

> He encouraged the leaders of the congregation to take a strong affirmative stand; he assisted them in their efforts to articulate their position; and he helped them to think through their educational ministry to the church.

> He helped create a feeling of stability and confidence among the majority of the members, who were primarily undecided about Alinsky.

> He comforted those who opposed Alinsky and enabled them to remain a part of the fellowship.

No new organizations or procedures were instituted for the purpose of dealing specifically with the Alinsky controversy. Since the congregation accepted Mr. Sharp's explanation that the matter was not a local issue, no need was expressed for a congregational vote. Although the session studied the issue thoroughly and decided how to handle the controversy, they did not vote on the presbytery's action. The normal channel of information, namely the pastor, was the one utilized. Since no opposing factions arose in the church, it seems that this arrangement successfully fulfilled its task. CORAR's area meeting was the only official meeting held at Christ Church.

The session also assisted in the process of communication. It invited all persons who wanted to express their views on Alinsky to a session meeting. Of the twelve persons who spoke, eleven were opposed. The session listened to all the presentations, but no discussion was held with the speakers.

At their annual retreat the church leaders had discussed the matter of controversy within the congregation and formulated some procedural guidelines for dealing with it. These procedures were to be employed for the dual purpose of allowing both direct action and education to take place. It appears that this strategy was well suited for Christ Church, for during the Alinsky dispute the church was able to confront a very controversial issue and move to resolution without being polarized.

The nature of the final decision was to trust the presbytery's bipartisan committee and the final vote of presbytery. The absence of a split within the congregation does not mean that the congregation unanimously supported the Alinsky proposal. In fact, our study indicated that perhaps as many as 40 percent of the laity were opposed to Alinsky, despite the strong support he received from church leaders. Although no vote was ever taken, the decision of Christ Church was to let presbytery resolve the issue. One delegate puts it this way: "The main thing which affected the way most people felt about the issue was that presbytery formed a bipartisan committee that commanded great respect. Most people here decided to go along with its recommendation."

Another fact that sheds light on the nature of Christ Church's decision is that they, like many other Presbyterian churches in the Bay Area, felt greatly relieved when the focal point of the final resolution was community organization and not Saul Alinsky. This fact raises the question of whether presbytery's final action eliminated the need for congregations to make a decision about Alinsky in particular.

Finally, we turn to the matter of membership involvement. About 250 people were deeply involved in the controversy. That is, they talked about it, read about it, attended the area meeting, and made a decision about how they felt. The focus of their involvement was through their own local congregation and not in outside groups such as CORAR and the Ad Hoc Appeals Committee.

CONSEQUENCES

1. *For the Church*

Measurable Effects. Using budget and membership as indicators, our study attempted to measure the amount of alienation that resulted in the congregation. Most informants agreed that fewer than ten people left the church because of the controversy. Although there was a significant drop in the 1967 budget, the budget proved to be a dubious indicator since it was impossible to determine how much of this decline was due specifically to the Alinsky controversy. The proposed budget for 1967 was $159,000; however, since only $118,000 was pledged, the new projected income for 1967 was lowered to $121,000. Even if one takes into consideration the possibility that the proposed figure of $159,000 was too high, the drop to $118,000 is significant because the income in 1966 was $150,-000. It is generally felt that the church's involvement in controversial issues was one factor in this decline; however, other factors are involved, especially the predictable letdown that follows an expensive building program and the rising cost of living.

Relationships Within the Church. Little or no evidence of alienation within Christ Church was discernible. In fact, the conflict had the effect of strengthening the relationships of those who actively supported Alinsky. We found no evidence of negative feelings toward CORAR or the General Council or presbytery.

Attitudes Toward Conflict. Most of our informants felt that the Alinsky controversy "proved that conflict over social issues need not be a destructive experience." They saw that it was possible for people to communicate and think rationally in an emotional situation. "We learned we could disagree and continue to have a church," was the way one man put it. Another man affirmed: "I learned that there were constructive aspects to conflict. Previously I had felt conflict was only destructive. I saw that conflict, if handled correctly, could produce greater awareness of social facts and enable people to formulate valid viewpoints." All our informants were firmly convinced that conflict over social issues would continue to be a greater reality in parish life. They believe that if the church is to deal creatively with this conflict, it must: (1) continue to discuss and debate controversial issues; (2) seek to deepen personal relationships among the members of the congregation; (3) provide a context where people can take an honest look at their own values and assumptions, and then call them into question.

Education. Quite clearly the lay people believe that their involvement in the Alinsky controversy produced a good deal of substantive education. They believe that the conflict forced people to learn new facts about poverty, community organization, and Saul Alinsky. A second effect was that many Presbyterians gained a new understanding of their church polity. As one man said, "We sure found out we weren't congregational."

Overall Impact on the Congregation. All our informants expressed the strong conviction that the Alinsky controversy was primarily a constructive experience for Christ Church. It was constructive in the sense that many members became more aware of pressing social problems in the Bay Area. Several persons, however, said they believed it was premature to judge whether the experience was constructive since the issue of Alinsky and community organization has yet to be resolved.

2. For the Community

Participation in the Alinsky controversy definitely affected the church's orientation toward social action. In the opinion of church leaders, by supporting the presbytery in its action, the church definitely became a congregation "that was not afraid of the hottest issues." (Just a few weeks after the Alinsky controversy the congregation was tackling explosive questions concerning migrant farm workers in the valley.) Church leaders believe that the experience has enabled them to see the close relationship between mission and education. They now see these two things as two dimensions of the same process.

To some extent interest in the mission of Christ Church waned once the issue was resolved; however, there is evidence that increased awareness of social need, which resulted from the experience, helped to set the stage for the congregation's decision to open a coffeehouse ministry for teen-agers in the community.

Another example of increased social involvement is the development of a spin-off organization. In the spring of 1966 a group of laymen from Christ Church, being dissatisfied with the fact that CORAR had not been able to bring Alinsky to Oakland, formed an ecumenical group called "Train an Oakland Organizer" (TOO). TOO's objective was to raise $10,000 in order to send a person from the Bay Area to an Alinsky-sponsored project for advanced training in community organization. This person was then to return to Oakland to engage in an intensive preorganization effort. At the time our study was completed, TOO had raised a substantial portion of the money; however, the program had slowed down considerably. The men active in TOO believe this is due largely to the air of uncertainty that has surrounded the whole idea of Alinsky's coming to Oakland.

5
Westminster

San Francisco's Westminster Presbyterian Church is a microcosm of most of the tensions, struggles, partial successes, and failures that characterize the church's recent experiments with worldly involvement.

Founded in 1878 with fifteen charter members, the congregation grew to a peak of over three thousand in 1961. A large proportion of its members have leaned toward a fundamentalist-pietist persuasion and a theological and political conservatism. From 1945 to 1962, Dr. Jonathan Oldman carried on a conservative ministry with two main emphases: Biblical preaching and foreign missions. Many new recruits from conservative backgrounds were attracted, as worship, prayer, fellowship, and harmony characterized the church's life. Under Dr. Oldman, Westminster members were "happy" with their church. Yet the congregation was not turned in on itself in self-centered isolation. In the foreign missions field, for example, Westminster provided a truly astonishing 10 percent of all American Presbyterian overseas personnel.

Toward the end of the fifties, Dr. Oldman began to realize that his own approach to Christianity was being challenged. He began to inform his parishioners of the need for "ministry at home," but he also realized that change within the congregation would be difficult for two reasons: the conservative habits associated with his pastorate and the fact that he was a "hometown boy" who was expected to comfort but not to challenge his old friends.

In 1962, Dr. Oldman was replaced by Dr. Edwin T. Hope, Westminster's current pastor. An intellectual with a historico-critical approach to the Bible and an intense social concern, he immediately began to lay the foundation for a thorough overhaul of Westminster's program. His overarching goal was to move the church into local mission. Dr. Hope's coming coincided with a series of domestic social upheavals including the civil rights movement, the beginnings of the open housing controversy, a school board recall election, and an outburst of student activism. The first phase of Dr. Hope's ministry was marked by bold and direct assaults on these issues. The effect was to burst the bubble of peace and harmony that had characterized Westminster under Dr. Oldman and to initiate an "upward spiral of controversy" that has continued ever since. For Westminster, the Alinsky debate must be seen in the context of Dr. Hope's long-term goal of moving the congregation from a pietistic foreign mission orientation to active local concern.

CHARACTERISTICS OF THE CONGREGATION

Socioeconomic Characteristics. At present, the membership of Westminster is 2,800, or roughly two hundred fewer than its 1961 peak. The members are preponderantly middle class. Income and housing are moderate to very good, but only a handful of members could be classified as wealthy. The educational level of the congregation varies widely due to a large segment of members drawn from the staff, faculty, and student body of a nearby university. Vocationally, Westminster's members are predominantly professional and white-collar workers. Politically, they are predominantly Republican. The church is currently engaged in a building program which, as population

studies indicate, must be completed before the church loses its
money base to adjacent suburban areas.

Situational Variables. In view of Dr. Hope's persistent
emphasis on "local mission," the church's location takes on
significance. This environmental situation presents two extremely important factors in Westminster's current life. On the
south is a large university and on the north and east an increasingly racially mixed residential area. Westminster's
neighborhood represents in miniature America's present urban
situation. Twenty years ago, the Lakeview section of San
Francisco was a residential "bedroom community" for businessmen working in downtown San Francisco. During the
fifties, however, Negro immigration into substantial portions
of Lakeview destroyed the community's middle-class comfort
and precipitated it into the caldron of urban problems. In
addition, Westminster's program is deeply affected by its
proximity to an academic center. On the one hand, the church
draws many members from the transient academic community. On the other hand, faced with urban change, its members
have tended to move to suburbia. Although many continue
their affiliation, it is likely that as Westminster accelerates its
urban action programs, these suburban families will transfer
their membership and thus undercut the church's financial
base. Since those who oppose Dr. Hope's program can wield
the threat of withdrawing membership and money, they have
a strong bargaining position.

Theological Orientation. In view of the recent shift in leadership from conservative to moderate/liberal, we expected a
broad range of theological variance. This prediction was borne
out. Although our informants unanimously acknowledged that
Westminster itself has become highly mission-oriented, their
definitions of the "nature of the church at large" ranged from a
predominantly spiritual-Biblical emphasis to a sociopolitical
emphasis. Only our two most conservative informants stated
that the church should not take stands on social and political
issues; the others ranged from "yes with discretion" to "of

course." Significantly, none of our informants denied that the church has a crucial role with reference to secular society, a role that demands involvement, awareness, and a willingness to carry Christian witness into the world. Although all our informants believed that the church should change *both* individuals and society, greater weight was placed on the former.

Drawing upon other survey studies of Westminster, we find that the congregation is now strongly in favor of inter-denominational and interfaith cooperation. Eighty-one percent of the members, for example, desire cooperation with other main-line Protestant denominations in the use of church plants. Four questions designed to test openness to change indicated that 74 percent of the members welcome innovation. The survey suggests, however, that the transfer from talk to action is not so clear-cut. Thus, 43 percent of the members indicated that the ministers should *not* speak their views on social and political issues. In addition, 42 percent opposed using the sanctuary for drama, modern dance, and the arts.

Deriving generalizations from such ambiguous data is, of course, highly dubious. Certainly, at the very least, the data support the conclusion that Westminster falls somewhere between the extremes of the polarized church. On the basis of the congregation's conservative background, this is evidence that some movement has taken place under Dr. Hope's pastorate. Indeed, most of our informants have moved substantially to the left of the attitude that prevailed when Dr. Oldman was pastor.

Pastoral Leadership. Westminster's size and wealth make possible the most interesting configuration of pastoral leadership found in any of our six churches, namely, the specialized multiple staff. Five permanent clergymen are on the staff. Dr. Hope is the senior pastor and has primary responsibility for preaching and overseeing the entire program. Rev. Robert Barton, "second in command," has secondary responsibility for worship services and primary responsibility for pastoral counseling. Mr. Barton is the most conservative of the five and plays an important role as spokesman for the congregation's conservative wing. Rev. Marcus Pressman, whose role in the Alinsky debate will be described extensively, is the "Minister for Urban Affairs." His sole duty is to develop effective ministries relating to urban problems in Lakeview and the greater Bay Area. In addition, Westminster has a fourth pastor specifically for the university students, and a fifth who administers a "ministry to the hippies."

This five-man staff comprises a "team" of specialists. Their theological range allows the church to work effectively with a diverse membership. Mr. Pressman's ability to pursue the implications of the Alinsky matter nearly full-time substantially facilitated Westminster's attempt to cope with the issue in a creative way. Dr. Hope, as coordinator, feels strongly that the staff must work as a team and support one another in the specialized projects.

Past Experience. Mr. Pressman refers to the last six years of Westminster's life as an "upward spiral of controversy." Our other informants also agree that 1962 marked a turning point. After arriving in 1962, Dr. Hope began attacking community problems. Among the early controversies, two stand out: an uproar over Dr. Hope's inviting a Communist pastor to speak at the church and a debate over a trip that one of the assistant pastors took to Hattiesburg, Mississippi.

The most intense uproar, however, concerned a sermon by Dr. Hope that ended with the statement that he intended to vote no on Proposition 14. This statement hit the congregation "like a ten megaton bomb." The outraged conservatives felt that their pastor had labeled a yes vote non-Christian. Controversy focused on whether the pastor should be allowed to speak out on such issues. During the shouting, some members left the church, and it became clear that the congregation was not ready to accept a frontal assault. The positive result of the uproar was that it surfaced the latent hostility and gave Dr. Hope a clearer reading of his parishioners' attitudes.

The effect of the Proposition 14 controversy was extremely significant: Dr. Hope realized that he would have to pull back. His purpose, after all, was to move the church into local mission, *not* merely to incite such an outrage that he would become a martyr at the hands of a conservative backlash. As he put it, "There is no point in driving off the bus and leaving the people standing at the corner." Dr. Hope's retreat, however, was not a headlong flight. On the contrary, still convinced that "the gospel must be applied to all of life," he initiated an extremely interesting delayed counterattack. Sensing the resistance of his members to local mission, Dr. Hope realized that the new challenge could not be successfully presented from the pulpit. Therefore, in 1966, he created the staff position entitled "Minister for Urban Affairs" and recruited Marcus Pressman for the post. In short, he created an action arm to carry forward the new worldly concerns. At the same time, he began to take a more delicate approach in the pulpit designed basically on the principle of alternating periods of "stretching" and "consolidation."

Working through Westminster's newly streamlined Department of Mission, Mr. Pressman proposed a flexible three-point program to focus on (1) communicating the gospel, (2) laying the basis for ecumenical cooperation in local mission, and (3) developing a keener social conscience among Westminster members. He initiated an educational program to reach as many members as possible. Its goal was to create a "lay task force in mission." After studies concerning target selection, the following programs were instigated: Task Force Literacy, focusing on person-to-person tutoring of illiterates; Task Force Friendship, focusing on visitation; Task Force Telephone, focusing on referrals to sources of assistance; and Task Force Big Brother, focusing on providing an adult friend for youth in poverty communities. In addition to these formal lay groups, which by the end of 1966 had roughly 320 workers, the Minister for Urban Affairs pursued his studies of the urban situation and the possibilities for new ministries.

Our discussion of internal developments at Westminster indicates the essential features of the "upward spiral of controversy" that has characterized the congregation since 1962. By early 1966 the congregation had been thoroughly exposed to internal conflict. The unanimous opinion of our informants, on the other hand, was that the members had had very little experience in dealing with race and poverty problems. Although prepared to handle the *process* of debate, the congregation was not prepared to discuss the substantive questions raised by the Alinsky proposal.

Structural Elements. In view of the competing concepts of Christian life at Westminster, it is important to understand the internal balance of power. According to Mr. Pressman, roughly half the congregation are totally unconcerned about current issues. Of the other half, one third are theologically and politically conservative, one third are theologically conservative but politically flexible, and one third are theologically in flux and politically liberal. Mr. Pressman feels that the middle third of the involved half are the key to the success or failure of his program.

In early 1966, just before CORAR made its proposal, the church was controlled by a conservative elite. This group, led by three extremely wealthy and powerful men, commanded a five to one majority of the session. The conservative elite was highly integrated and had an effective, although informal, organization. It met together frequently, usually at social gatherings. During the same period, the visible liberals, comprising roughly one sixth of the congregation, were almost wholly unorganized. They tended to gather in several of the church's "clubs," but their agenda was purely "talk and fellowship." Thus, although a substantial segment of the congregation had taken up the challenge presented by Dr. Hope and Mr. Pressman, they were not yet solidified into a counterelite capable of resistance. In addition, the liberals themselves were not ready for Saul Alinsky.

Notes Mr. Pressman: "The last few years at Westminister

present a classic example of a traditional church's trying to
fight its way into action." Is the battle succeeding or failing?
Both Dr. Hope and Mr. Pressman feel that they have had fair
success in moving a substantial segment of the congregation
toward readiness for social action. (One liberal session member, for example, stated that, in the early sixties, vote on the
session was 32–1 against him, whereas at present, the breakdown is more like 25–8.) Another segment of the membership,
however, and a wealthy one at that, are viewed as chronically
unwilling to accept Worldly Christianity. Thus, during the
very period in which support for new ministries has been
growing, a powerful opposition has been developing in the
form of an angry conservative backlash. At present, a critical
point has been reached, and the fate of the program is hanging
in the balance.

DYNAMICS OF DECISION-MAKING

In April, 1966, Saul Alinsky was injected into the life of
this changing congregation. For the congregation at large, the
news was broken by the post-April 12 coverage in the Bay
Area newspapers. The congregation's original response has
been characterized as a groundswell of anger. Mr. Pressman,
for example, received roughly fifty letters and one hundred
phone calls and had twenty-five personal appointments with
irate parishioners. Despite several years of preparation in dealing with social issues, the members were not ready for Alinsky,
and their initial response was at least 90 percent in opposition.
A recent sociological study shows a solid 71 percent veto of
Alinsky. Nevertheless, the past experience with urban mission
did have at least one salutary effect: it prevented a destruc-
tively explosive outburst of hostility. In fact, while emphasizing the intense fear, horror, and bitterness felt by many
members, our informants were nearly unanimous in the judgment that the Alinsky dispute should be viewed as merely one
in a series of conflict situations. Furthermore, the general im-

pression was that the controversy comprised a secondary—albeit important—aspect of a long-term crisis which had actually climaxed earlier in the Proposition 14 explosion. Thus in this particular case, CORAR's expectations were correct: Proposition 14 had laid the basis for a more rational handling of the Alinsky issue.

The rapid response of the Westminster staff also helped to keep the reaction from getting out of hand. Groundwork for this response was laid before April 12. As a member of CORAR, Mr. Pressman had received advance warning of the proposed action, and he found himself opposed to hiring Alinsky. Thus, when the notice of the emergency meeting arrived, the matter was discussed at a specially called session meeting, and Mr. Pressman took charge of an informal steering committee to prepare for April 12. Westminster delegates, although not instructed by the session, went to the presbytery meeting prepared to resist the CORAR proposal. When their efforts failed and the measure passed, the staff moved quickly to confront the issue within the congregation and to prevent a destructive conflict. On the first Sunday after April 12, the assistant pastor preached a sermon that the liberals now refer to as the notorious "Bob Barton statement." The gist of the message was that the Westminster staff opposed the April 12 action and would make every effort to rescind it. This relieved much anxiety. Reassured that its leaders would go to the barricades to oppose Alinsky, the congregation began to relax with the expectation that the proposal would be killed. Thus, the Westminster fever chart showed an early peak and then a relatively rapid decline.

The staff strategy, however, was not merely to "put out the fire." Far from it. On the contrary, the staff recognized the post April 12 situation as a context in which creative action might be possible. As Dr. Hope put it, the goal was to channel the aroused emotion into a search for alternatives. The staff was genuinely opposed to Alinsky on the ground that he had not improved his tactics for twenty-five years and had consequently become obsolete and ineffective. Nevertheless, they were eager to move the congregation into some form of appropriate and useful involvement in the race and poverty area. Thus, the plan was neither to suppress the issue nor to allow a destructive backlash, but rather to use the anxiety created by the Alinsky threat for the purpose of developing an alternative program. Dr. Hope sought to convey this message: "The matter arose because of a terrible need. But don't blow off your energy in anger. The question is *not* Alinsky or nothing. It's Alinsky or something better." Ultimately, this plan led to an ambitious job-training institute in which Westminster, and particularly its Minister for Urban Affairs, played a significant role.

Structurally, the discussion of the Alinsky issue was carried on through a variety of channels. Communication to the entire congregation was handled in three ways: first, through Mr. Barton's sermon and other statements from the pulpit; second, through announcements in the church's news bulletin; and third, through an open forum discussion held in the social hall. The latter device had been previously used in the Proposition 14 controversy, and it drew over one hundred members. Communication to the congregation as a whole, however, was not the principal method for carrying forward the debate. Mr. Pressman's opinion, for example, is that with a membership as large and diverse as Westminster's, effective discussion must take place in the smaller and more specialized groups and committees. Thus, the main forum for debate was the various church subcommittees. The session, for example, considered the matter and reached a decision to call for a reconsideration of the April 12 action. In addition, there were discussions in the Department of Mission, in Sunday morning study classes (including the Women's Study Program), in a Young Married People's group, and in the Liberals' Club. Appraisals of the discussion varied widely: some liberals felt that there was little effective debate and, in fact, no real forum for debate at all; others opined that the debate had been open, interesting,

and constructive. Although more than half of the congregation
were negligibly involved in the Alinsky issue, the minority
who were exercised and talking represented "the heart of the
church." It is safe to say that the controversy evoked an unusually high degree of membership involvement. Nevertheless,
only normal and authorized procedures were used.

Since the content of the discussion was so diverse, it is
difficult to isolate any single definition of the situation. To a
large extent, of course, the debate focused on Alinsky. Even
here, however, there was no consensus concerning the critical
questions. Considerable attention was directed to the substantive question of need among racial and poverty communities and appropriate methods for dealing with it. In this
regard, the staff's effort to focus on articulating alternatives to
Alinsky seems to have had a salutary effect. There was a
general distrust of Alinsky's methods, particularly his use of
bitterness, organized lawlessness, and hatred. Skepticism was
also expressed concerning Alinsky's tendency to undermine
existing patterns of Negro leadership and his lack of permanent stake in the community. In short, for many members of
the congregation, the focus of discussion was how to deal with
the racial situation, and the consensus which reflected the
staff's opinion, was that Alinsky's methods were obsolete and
would likely produce more harm than good. Another segment
of church members, however, fastened on Alinsky's personal
style. They were outraged by Alinsky's atheism and vulgarity.
These issues of personal style, however, did not play the overwhelmingly important role that they tended to play in some of
the more conservative congregations.

Other issues figured significantly in the discussion. There
was some anger and bitterness concerning the apparent attempt by CORAR to railroad the matter through an unprepared presbytery. One of our informants suggested that this
issue was hot at the beginning but that, over time, interest
shifted to other matters. There was concern about the size of
the sum offered and about the possibility that the church

would be liable for Alinsky's subsequent activities. Some members feared that the presence of Alinsky might lead to riots. The congregation was split over the desirability of community organization: the staff was fairly supportive of the tactic, but for some members community organization represented an attempt to go too far too fast. As in the other churches, the broad question of church involvement in social action was seen as the overarching ideological question involved, but at Westminster the debate seems to have focused mainly on the specifics of the CORAR proposal and possible alternatives, rather than on the abstract question concerning the church's role in the world.

As we have said, the staff had some success in its attempt to focus discussion on the articulation of alternatives. There was substantial agreement on the urgent necessity for some sort of action in response to the needs of racial minorities. The discussion of alternatives, therefore, focused on defining the precise nature of needs and appropriate responses. A general consensus was reached that need should be defined in terms of specific problems and goals such as housing, job training, and education and that responses should focus on solving these particular problems. As a result of these decisions, members aligned with Job Corps, an existing private agency for job training and placement, which had been foundering and in danger of going under. Mr. Pressman adopted the agency as a major point of concern, and with resources and support from Westminster members undertook to revive and improve the program. In the opinion of those members who have followed the developments, the effort has met with impressive success. The pastors used a "division of labor" in managing the conflict. Dr. Hope tended to take a back seat, but when he did step forward, he attempted to educate and to counteract outside factors that were whipping up emotion. Mr. Barton, who was more strongly opposed to the CORAR action than the others, calmed the more conservative members by promising to fight against the CORAR action. Finally, Mr.

Pressman had the primary responsibility for interpreting the CORAR proposal. The general feeling, apart from some liberal dissidents who felt that the pastors had been evasive, was that the staff did a supreme job of reconditioning the parishioners to be open to the necessity of taking some sort of constructive action.

CONSEQUENCES

1. For the Church

Measurable Effects. As we have said, Westminster's recent history has involved a series of experiments and reactions giving rise to an upward spiral of controversy. The Alinsky dispute is merely one incident in a long-term development. It is difficult to attribute specific consequences to this issue alone apart from the general trend in the congregation's life.

In the first place, although there has been a substantial loss in membership and pledges, there is no way to isolate the particular portion stemming from the Alinsky controversy. Note that over the last six years, there has been a steady membership decline. Estimates run as high as three to five hundred turnover due primarily to increased emphasis on social action. As for those who withdrew during 1966, the general feeling is that the Alinsky matter may have been the straw that broke the camel's back, but it probably was not solely responsible. Similarly, there has been a significant and alarming reduction in pledges. One relatively wealthy conservative informant, for example, stated that he has cut his pledge in half, but he cited the Alinsky incident as simply one of many factors leading to his decision. Mr. Pressman estimates that at least a $30,000 loss can be attributed directly to the Alinsky dispute. The overall effect of the budget loss is that the congregation found itself running nearly $50,000 behind what the staff considered to be a bare bones operating requirement for the first half of 1967. Church leaders are deeply concerned about the budget situation, but they feel that the crisis was peaking

and that the survival of the local mission program would be
decided in the near future. It is also hypothesized by some
members that, had the CORAR action gone through, a catastrophic loss of both members and money would have occurred.

Relationships Within the Church. The effect of the Alinsky
controversy on relationships among Westminster members and
within the Presbyterian Church at large was minimal. Mr.
Pressman, the Minister for Urban Affairs, appears to have improved his position in the eyes of a large segment of the congregation by virtue of his role in the discussion. Dr. Hope and
the session, however, elicited some critical fire from the more
liberal elements for not taking a more decisive stand. Most of
our informants felt that CORAR's reputation suffered in the
eyes of the majority of members, and some sensed a slight
deterioration in Westminster's relation to the national Presbyterian Church. On the other hand, effects on relationships
among Westminster members were negligible.

Attitudes Toward Conflict. Westminster members are being
conditioned to accept conflict as a reality of parish life. The
strong, conservative response to Dr. Hope's pronouncement
on Proposition 14 may be viewed as the last attempt of the
conservative wing to "muzzle" the staff, and it did force Dr.
Hope to pull back to some degree. Events since 1964, however,
have compelled the congregation to recognize that the pastors
will speak out and that there is no avoiding confrontation with
social issues and conflict. In this sense, Westminster is tending
toward some liberal orientation in its internal processes of
discussion and decision-making. Dr. Hope, however, clearly
recognizes that the battle is far from won: many members still
shy away from conflict, and the church lacks an adequate
forum for voicing controversial views.

The Alinsky controversy was just one step in Westminster's
long-term lesson in facing conflict. Although the original reaction to the newspapers and TV threatened to get out of
control and produce a backlash, the staff was able to steer the

controversy back to the substantive issues and bring it to an acceptable conclusion. Nevertheless, half of our informants declared that the Alinsky controversy achieved nothing in terms of getting the congregation to accept conflict as a reality of parish life.

Education. Once again, the educational effects of the Alinsky controversy cannot be separated from the long-range educational process that has been taking place within the Westminster congregation. Conservative informants felt that very little education had taken place and that members had, by and large, been unaffected. Moderates, on the other hand, tended to feel that "quite a lot" of education had been achieved. Areas of education mentioned include a general increase in awareness of pressing needs, a sense that something has to be done, a recognition of the dignity of opposing viewpoints, and a sharper understanding of alternative approaches to the problem. Some feeling was expressed that the situation was like "throwing a child into the water" and that it may have had a negative long-term educational effect. A narrow majority of our informants claimed constructive education on the topics of the church in social action, poverty problems, community organization, and the methods of Saul Alinsky. A substantial minority, however, felt that no education had taken place on these issues, and a few suggested that the issue had yielded negative results.

Overall Impact on the Congregation. As to the overall effect of the controversy, there was an even split of opinion. Half of our respondents stated that the effect had been healthy, while the other half felt it had been destructive, and Mr. Pressman said that it had been both. Furthermore, there is no apparent correlation between the political and theological attitudes of the informants and their appraisals of the effects of the controversy. Nearly all the moderates and liberals among our informants, however, recommended more of this type of controversy as a healthy program for the church.

2. For the Community

We have already discussed the ambiguous effect of the Alinsky debate on the attitudes of Westminster members toward race and poverty problems. Moderates and liberals sense an increased understanding of needs and willingness to take action. Mr. Pressman, for example, agrees that the congregation has moved from "conservative" to "moderate" on these issues. Conservatives, on the other hand, speaking perhaps only for themselves, claim that the debate was counterproductive: it alienated the sympathy that had developed during the civil rights movement.

One important consequence concerns spin-off programs. The staff, as we have noted, made a special effort to focus discussion on "alternatives to Alinsky" rather than "Alinsky or not." They interpreted CORAR's action as a genuine, albeit mistaken, attempt to respond to an extremely difficult problem, namely the urban ghetto. As a result, increased support was generated for at least four programs: Task Force Literacy, Task Force Telephone, Task Force Big Brother, and Job Corps. Job Corps remains the most impressive of these spin-off programs. During 1966, Mr. Pressman made Job Corps one of his special projects and attempted to generate ecumenical support for it. Since that time, Job Corps has made notable gains in placing its graduates. Mr. Pressman, however, suggests an interesting belated development: once the threat of Alinsky faded, the members of Westminster began to withdraw their support from Job Corps, and the overall effect may have been to make the corps's task more difficult than before. A final spin-off from the Alinsky debate was staff involvement in the West San Francisco Urban Planning Department, a committee of clergymen and laymen attempting to study urban needs and coordinate the church's responses to them.

In view of its unusually large and diverse membership, Westminster represents perhaps every segment of contemporary Protestantism except the radical left. It has a large number of apathetic and uninformed members, a substantial and powerful conservative wing, a significant moderate group, and an unorganized and ineffective but somewhat sizable liberal segment. Thus, the attempt of Westminster to "fight its way into local mission" reflects clearly the struggles of the church at large. The staff is politically astute and has been able to achieve a division of labor that enhances its chances for effectiveness. Study of the church reveals that staff efforts have had a significant effect. Over the last seven years the congregation has shifted from a conservative to a moderate stance.

Nevertheless, as with the church at large, the attempt to move the church into action has met with only a measure of success. For one thing, there appears to be a substantial segment who simply do not share the new image of local mission. Within Westminster, the conservative elite has become increasingly hostile and is organized to fight further changes. In addition, this group is sufficiently wealthy and powerful to exert pressure at the fiscal juncture. Secondly, although a large proportion of former conservatives have become more moderate, these individuals appear to be unorganized and negligibly action-oriented. The avowedly "liberal" group within the congregation, for example, has no intention and apparently no desire to be anything more than a discussion and recreation club. In fact, one of its leaders expressed an unwillingness to organize further for fear of conservative reaction.

Will the shift to Worldly Christianity succeed? The outcome is genuinely in doubt. Mr. Pressman has expressed real worries about his program. Unless the budget situation improves, he feels that he may be merely destroying the institution rather than moving it into a new form of life. Dr. Hope is generally optimistic. His opinion is that the experiment is succeeding, but that the results will not be in for another decade. In any case, the belief of both the pastors and many of the members is that the outcome at Westminster will be a fairly accurate barometer of whether the church at large can succeed in its worldly involvement. Failure *may* mean that the parish is not a viable instrument for social action. Success, on the other hand, would represent a very hopeful sign for the advocates of Worldly Christianity. Certainly, if the handling of the Alinsky controversy is any test, Westminster has come a long way from its former affinity to Churchly Christianity.

6
Fargo

Fargo Presbyterian Church was badly split over the Alinsky proposal. At the outset nearly half the members were opposed to presbytery's action, while the other half supported it. This conflict was never resolved and seventy members left the church. Although the Alinsky controversy was a very painful experience for those involved, knowledge of what happened here should help us understand the variety of responses to the presbytery's move to be involved in the world.

Fargo, California, a middle-class city with 60,000 population, is adjacent to Oakland. Primarily a residential community, it contains several large tracts of small, two- and three-bedroom homes. The church, founded in 1952, is located in one of these housing tracts and grew with the community. Between 1955 and 1961 expansion was rapid and church programs were well supported. Benevolence giving was nearly 30 percent of the total budget.

Both the pastor, who has served the church since it began, and the members agree that a slow decline in church vitality began in 1962. Some call the period from 1955 to 1961 "the really good years" and from 1962 through 1966 the "period of disillusionment." The last portion of the church plant, the sanctuary, was built in 1962 at a cost of $84,000. This project left the church heavily in debt. Then came a series of social crises. First, there was Proposition 14. The pastor worked hard in the community to defeat Proposition 14. Some members left the church, but most of the people silently resented his activity. Then came Selma in 1965 and Alinsky in 1966.

One indicator of the impact which these events had on Fargo Church is the budget. In 1964 the total budget was $42,700; however, in 1965 it had dropped to $40,500 and by 1966 the budget was down to $32,700—a drop of nearly $8,000. Since the budget for 1967 was not expected to reach $30,000, the church sold the parsonage in order to meet its financial obligations. Attendance at all church functions declined. In 1962 attendance at three Sunday worship services totaled over 300, but now two services draw less than 100. Church leaders claim it is almost impossible to recruit adults for leadership positions in the church. At least twenty families left the church after the Alinsky controversy. Despite these signs of decline, the pastor Rev. Jack Heart, and a few current leaders maintain that the small group of people who remain at Fargo Church are deeply committed to the idea of a church related to the world. They feel the church has experienced a sense of renewal. Hopefully, our analysis will shed some light on the validity of that claim.

CHARACTERISTICS OF THE CHURCH

Socioeconomic Characteristics. Most of the members of Fargo Church are middle class, with an average income between $8,000 and $9,000 a year. Occupations include: blue-collar workers, office workers, small businessmen, and teachers. Less than half of the congregation has more than a high school education.

Theological Orientation. Since we were aware of two opposite views toward the Alinsky controversy within Fargo, representatives of both groups were interviewed. Our data reflect this split situation. We will refer to the group that sup-

ported the Alinsky proposal as the "proponents" and the opposing group as the "opponents." The following are typical
responses of each group to a set of questions:

ISSUE	OPPONENTS	PROPONENTS
What is the nature of the church?	It is a community that teaches what Christ said and what the Bible says in order to help his people.	It is a community called together by the Holy Spirit who have responsibility of exploring the world and finding the points of tension and then putting itself between the combatants.
What is the purpose of the Fargo congregation?	To produce a better world by making strong Christians.	To become aware of the forces in our society that keep people from being the creatures they can become —to locate the mechanisms of isolation and then work to produce community.
Does this church serve the larger community?	Yes, we do. We have a good youth program and the pastor makes himself available to the community.	Some do, yes. But not the congregation as a whole. Most are just Sunday Christians.
What is the church's relation to secular society?	It should teach Christ and the Bible. We can do this best by being faithful witnesses.	The church is like a voltmeter. It can measure society's potential. It should point out how far society has to go in realizing its ideals. It should be deeply involved in renewing society.

ISSUE	OPPONENTS	PROPONENTS
Should the church take stands on political issues?	No. Such matters are for the individual to decide. Anyway, the minister is a theologian and not a politician.	Yes, definitely. However, the pastor must be careful that he doesn't attempt to speak for the whole church.
Should the church focus on changing individuals or society?	Change the individual and you will have a good society.	The church should try to do both. The main thing is to get into the confusion and see where God is at work building community.
What should the church teach its members concerning their involvement in race and poverty issues?	Teach God's Word and the rest follows. If you help make people Christian, they'll know what is right.	The church should help people make the connections between the gospel and the realities of life. It must deal with facts and talk about specific cases.

The responses of the proponents seem more theologically alert than those of the opponents. Since no significant educational or personal distinctions exist between the individuals, much of the difference arises from the fact that all the proponents have been involved in Parish Communicant Education (PCE) at Fargo Church. PCE is a program where laymen gather in small groups and use denominational materials to wrestle in depth with their own theological questions. Experience in PCE enabled the proponents to more adequately formulate and articulate their own positions.

Obviously there is a significant difference between the attitudes of the two groups. The opponents definitely reflect a pietistic attitude. They are basically interested in the individual's need for salvation and in acquiring salvation through an experience of faith. The proponents, however, tend toward a Christian humanism. Their primary focus is on how the church can work in the world to create community and wholeness.

Pastoral Leadership. Since 1962 much of the pastor's ministry has been spent in attempting to resolve differences between various factions within the church. This reconciling activity, however, took place at a rather superficial level. Neither Mr. Heart nor the congregation was able to resolve the basic differences. Mr. Heart, a rather quiet and unassuming man, is definitely committed to a "ministry of reconciliation to all men"; however, he was unable, prior to 1966, to get the congregation to discuss such matters seriously. The conservatives in the congregation were content to allow him to preach on social issues as long as he didn't get the congregation itself involved.

Past Experience. Since the founding of Fargo Church, constant tension has existed between the two wings of the congregation. This tension usually surfaced in discussions concerning the church's stewardship programs. One group felt that missions should come first and that the church should give at least one third of its budget for benevolence. The other group gave priority to the building up of the fellowship, and hence advocated spending more money on local programs. Even before the social controversies erupted, conflicting opinions regarding the church's purpose and directions were rampant. This tug-of-war between the mission group and the maintenance group was never resolved, and, in fact, it became worse as time went on. Mr. Heart comments on his efforts to cope with the problem. "I have attempted to deal with this split. I've tried to lift up the mission of the church through education and discussion, but I can't seem to rise above the tension. Until Proposition 14 came along I thought we were making progress, but that and the Alinsky thing scared many people. Now many just want to 'play house.' Even some of the people who had favored mission reacted against Proposition 14 and Alinsky."

Alienation increased considerably when the congregation faced Proposition 14. Mr. Heart took a strong stand against 14, while the rest of the congregation, including the session, either remained quiet or favored the Proposition. Mr. Heart preached several times on the issue and only aroused resentment. Many felt he was trying "to tell the church how to vote." In an effort to clear the air, the pastor organized a series of forum meetings to stimulate debate. For the most part, however, they were simply ignored. The largest number in attendance was twelve. At least ten people left the church due to the pastor's stand. During 1965 and 1966 Mr. Heart continued to address himself to social issues, especially urban poverty, civil rights, and war. This naturally aggravated those who felt the church should stay out of politics; however, a small group agreed openly with the pastor and supported his position. These supporters emerged from what was left of the group previously described as having advocated mission over against maintenance.

One of the most dynamic structures in the church is the Parish Communicant Education (PCE) program. Groups consist of eight to twelve persons who meet together once a week for thirty-six weeks over a four-year period. The first year curriculum is a study of the Old Testament; the second year focuses on the New Testament; the third year discusses theology; and the fourth year studies worship and work. An interesting feature of PCE is that it is entirely a lay operation. Its purpose is to enable laymen themselves to think through their theological questions. All the participants in PCE were highly enthusiastic about it. Here is a typical comment: "I feel PCE has been one of the most significant things that ever happened to me at church. I have learned so much. Just six weeks after our group began to meet, we had a very heated discussion over the devil. We never did resolve the disagreement, but we did come to accept each other. From then on our group was more like a family. We felt as though we could say anything."

Two PCE groups existed at the time of the Alinsky controversy. Everyone in the PCE groups became deeply involved. Significantly, although not everyone in PCE groups favored the proposal, none of the opposing PCE members left the church. As we shall see later, most of those who were bitterly opposed to the proposal did finally leave the congregation.

Opponents of the Alinsky proposal criticized the educational program. They resented the fact that a Bible class, which had been taught by a retired minister, had been dropped. They claimed the pastor had it eliminated because it took too many people out of church. The opponents, even before the Alinsky controversy, felt alienated from worship because of "the political nature of the sermons" and alienated from the education program because "their class" had been eliminated. There were no programs in the educational structure that provided for persons from the two divergent groups to meet together and discuss their differences.

With the exception of an occasional congregational meeting, the session seems to be the only place where differences could be aired. However, the level of discussion there usually did not reach beyond such "practical" matters as finances, programs, etc. Except for an occasional outburst, very little hostility was expressed openly between opponents and proponents. They worshiped, fellowshiped, and transacted business together; yet, underlying these activities there was a latent feeling of estrangement. The opponents had very little knowledge of Bay Area race and poverty problems before the Alinsky conflict. What awareness they did have came from the mass media. None of them knew anything about community organization, Saul Alinsky, or the presbytery's Commission on Religion and Race. On the other hand, the proponents had a much greater awareness of specific problems in the Bay Area. Their awareness came from Mr. Heart's sermons, involvement in PCE, and discussions in an earlier race relations class. They also had some familiarity with Saul Alinsky.

From 1964 to 1966, Fargo Church did not sponsor any major social action programs. There was some individual and small group involvement. One of the PCE groups established a relationship with a Negro congregation. Several people were involved in a ministry to migrant workers in the valley. Many members contributed to support a ministry to the "down and out" in Oakland. Finally, the pastor and the subsequent leader of the proponents belonged to two local groups that were attempting to create a more favorable climate for race relations in Fargo. None of the opponents was active in race relations.

Structural Elements. In 1964 the session refused to stand with Mr. Heart on Proposition 14. However, in 1966 they chose to stand with him in favoring the Alinsky proposal. This situation reflects the fact that a new leadership elite was in control of the session. Virtually no communication existed between the new leaders who had gained control and the older elites who still held some important posts. It is also clear that the new leaders did not feel entirely secure in their position, and that the older leaders were not ready to completely relinquish their positions in the decision-making machinery of the church.

Dynamics of Decision-Making

"A violent outburst of feelings"—this definition of an explosion aptly characterized Fargo Church's response to the news that presbytery had voted to support Saul Alinsky. Smoldering resentment within the congregation was fanned into a raging fury. Five phases of the explosion may be delineated.

The first phase includes the events that occurred from the presbytery's vote on Tuesday through the following Saturday. On Wednesday a special session meeting discussed how the issue should be presented to the congregation. During this discussion only two elders spoke out against the proposal. It was decided to have the delegate to presbytery explain the action during the Sunday worship services. On Friday and Saturday of the same week, Mr. Heart received several calls from members who were very upset by what they had read in the *Oakland Tribune*. He told them to remain calm and the whole thing would be explained at Sunday worship.

The second phase of Fargo's explosive response took place on Sunday morning, April 17. It is noteworthy that even the worship life of this community reflected its split personality and that the very structure of worship tended to keep the two groups from interacting. Fargo Church had two worship services. The nine o'clock service was designed as an experiment to test new forms of worship. Communion was celebrated every Sunday and the whole atmosphere of the hour was one of intimacy and informality. Only a small group of thirty-five to forty normally attended. Commenting on this service, one woman noted: "Some of us, because of our involvement with the in-depth Bible discussion groups and PCE, prefer the relaxed and personal atmosphere. Of the eight people in our PCE group, seven usually go to the first service. I would think that very few people there would object to the church's involvement in politics." Her last observation was accurate, for when the Alinsky proposal was explained, there were questions, but no explosion.

The violent reaction came during the eleven o'clock service, which follows the traditional Presbyterian worship pattern and is attended by most of the members.

Mr. Heart said he felt the congregation that came to the second service that morning was "smoldering." Mr. Rip, delegate to presbytery, explained the Alinsky proposal and why he voted in its favor. Then came a violent outburst of resentment against presbytery's decision to support Alinsky. Many who spoke were so angry they were trembling and crying. Tempers flared and some members walked out before the meeting ended. One of the men who walked out said: "I think most people were horrified at what they heard. I was flabbergasted!"

The two weeks following that explosive Sunday meeting comprise the third phase of Fargo's response. Those opposed to Alinsky organized themselves. They held meetings, drafted letters, carried on a telephone campaign, and attended meetings held by the Ad Hoc Appeals Committee. Their efforts were largely directed at the local congregation rather than at the presbytery. Specifically, they pressed for a congregational meeting where the issue could be discussed and voted on.

The response of the church's official leadership to these organizational efforts by the opposition constitutes the fourth phase. A forum-type meeting was arranged to present facts and to provide an opportunity for expression of viewpoints. Also a special session meeting was set for hearing grievances.

The fifth and final phase can again be described as an explosion. Opponents of the proposal felt the forum meeting "was stacked against them" from the beginning. Later, when the session refused to designate its special meeting as an official congregational meeting that could entertain a vote, most of the opposition group (about seventy people) left the church.

Debate at Fargo focused upon two issues: Alinsky and the internal methods of handling the controversy. Those who opposed Alinsky felt "the Christian Church could not do business with an atheist who preaches hate and creates hostility." Proponents agreed that in the beginning Alinsky's character was the chief issue. Mr. Rip noted: "We tried to focus the controversy on the ghetto problems and the Negro's need for power, but the opponents would not accept that idea. We always ended up discussing Alinsky." The proponents favored Alinsky because "his type of community organization seemed to be successful in bringing about change where change seemed impossible." They were not bothered by his personality or his tactics, and they indicated that Alinsky was "a real servant of the church's ministry to minority groups."

The opponents said they approved of community organization and assisting Negroes, but it was Alinsky they were against. However, they defined community organization as the network of existing charitable and government agencies established to assist the underprivileged. When community organization is defined as a process of establishing an indigenous sociopolitical power base in the ghetto community, the opponents objected because "it gets away from changing the individual."

As time went on, another issue surfaced and became as central as the Alinsky issue. The opposition was very angry at the way the controversy was handled in the local congregation. One man expressed a typical feeling: "For me the whole thing was that they took us. They didn't tell us about this program or what they were planning. I didn't know anything about Alinsky before they told us about him at church, but I couldn't be objective then. They used our questions to beat us down rather than to inform us." Opponents were angry at Mr. Heart and the session for giving insufficient warning, for making the announcement during a worship service, for having Mr. Rip rather than Mr. Heart make the announcement, and for not calling a congregational meeting and allowing the congregation to vote.

In the end, the issue became strictly a local one, namely, who has the decision-making authority in this congregation?

Let us turn our attention to the meetings of the opposition group. Three sessions were held in the homes of various members to discuss the plan of action. At the first meeting, members listened to a tape of an Alinsky speech and heard reports from those who had attended the Ad Hoc Appeals Committee's breakfast meetings. An outcome of this meeting was to ask Mr. Heart and Mr. Rip to attend the next meeting and discuss the Alinsky matter. After accepting the invitation, Mr. Heart discovered he had previously agreed to an out-of-town speaking engagement. He was therefore unable to meet with the group. However, a group of thirty-five did meet. At this second meeting they drafted a very strong letter protesting the stand taken by the pastor and the session, and they also criticized the way in which the pastor was performing his ministry (i.e., taking sides, too many political sermons, etc.). Before mailing the letter to other members, the opponents sought again to meet with Mr. Heart.

The opposition group's third meeting was a "very painful and tense affair." Forty-eight people in attendance presented Mr. Heart a strong letter that had been drafted. He disapproved of its sharp language and indicated that the charges made could have serious repercussions for the laymen making them. The group then expressed their dissatisfaction with the way Mr. Heart had handled the whole situation and demanded that he call a congregational meeting. Mr. Heart replied that there was no point in calling a meeting because the issue was ultimately a presbytery matter and not in the hands of the local congregation. This interpretation, however, did not square with what members had heard at the Ad Hoc breakfast meetings. They insisted on the right to petition presbytery for reconsideration and they demanded a congregational vote on the matter. At this point Mr. Heart said he preferred not to see that happen, for it would split the congregation. After lengthy discussion, a compromise was reached. The group agreed not to distribute the letter and Mr. Heart agreed to call a special meeting of the session open to all those desiring to speak on the Alinsky matter.

Over 130 people attended the special meeting, the largest number in several years to attend an official church function. Presentations were limited to three minutes. An opposition statement was introduced which listed the complaints and called for a congregational vote and election of a delegate other than Mr. Rip to send to presbytery's June meeting. After this statement was read, discussion followed. Near the end of the meeting, someone called for a vote. Despite Mr. Heart's reminder that the session was not an officially constituted congregational meeting, a show of hands was called for. It indicated an overwhelming opposition to the Alinsky proposal.

Recall that one of the opposition's demands was that the session should send another delegate to the June presbytery meeting. They felt that Mr. Rip failed to represent the congregation's thinking. The night after the special meeting, however, the session voted 6 to 5 to send Mr. Rip. To the opposition this was a "direct slap in the face." After this decision most of the opposition group's members decided they could no longer remain in the Fargo congregation.

In summary, we may conclude that normal procedures for decision-making at Fargo Church were followed. The session elected the delegate to presbytery and he voted "his conscience" there. On the local level the session and the pastor decided the policy that would be followed in handling the controversy. No special committees were set up. On the other hand, new organizational features did appear as a result of the congregation's attempt to handle the conflict. The special announcement in the worship service, the forum meeting, and the special session meeting were efforts by the proponents to affirm their decision and to maintain the unity of the congregation. The informal meetings held by the opposition and the special meeting they demanded with the session were efforts to change the session's decision.

If a vote had been taken, the likelihood is that the congregation would not have supported the presbytery's action. Because of this fact and because he feared a vote would split the congregation down the middle, Mr. Heart did not favor voting. Yet he knew that the opposition felt they had no voice in the official decision-making process and so he attempted to redress the imbalance by creating channels for the opposition to express opinions. However, this technique did not succeed, for the opposition felt that the session and the pastor were only listening to them in order to maintain organizational unity. They saw their speeches would not really affect the decisions of the session, the pastor, and the lay delegate. Realizing this fact, they finally left the congregation. In short, Mr. Heart failed in his dual objective to support Alinsky and to avoid a split.

Membership involvement in the controversy was unusually high at Fargo Church. Since the congregation is not too large (450) and since there was considerable pressure toward polarized positions, this fact is not surprising. Our data show that 25 percent of the congregation were deeply involved, 50 percent were moderately involved, and 25 percent were only negligibly involved. All informants agreed that no other issue had ever generated such widespread and intense congregational participation.

Officially Fargo Church supported the Alinsky proposal. Their presbytery delegation voted for it, and their session endorsed the action. Unofficially another decision was made in the church—roughly seventy members decided they could no longer tolerate "not being heard" and they withdrew from the congregation.

An examination of Fargo Church's membership roll, budget, and internal programs shows the extent of alienation resulting from the Alinsky controversy. Seventy members, or 15 percent of the total membership, withdrew from the church. Of those who left, at least twenty had been very active in various church programs and had been generous contributors. So their departure significantly affected church budget and programs. In 1966 the budget dropped nearly 20 percent from the previous years and it was expected to drop again in 1967. The programs that suffered the most were worship services, adult education, and youth activities. At least two youth groups were discontinued because no adult sponsors could be found.

CONSEQUENCES

1. For the Church

Relationships Within the Church. The controversy had obviously a powerful effect on relationships within the congregation. Those who withdrew felt disappointed and hostile toward the pastor and other members. Despite strong opposition to Alinsky, some members found they could remain in the fellowship and still work with people who held different views. One man commented that "it felt better to know where everyone stood."

Although considerable alienation was experienced, it was also discovered that relationships were strengthened among proponents of the proposal and between them and the pastor. The bitter personal attack by the opposition on both Mr. Rip and Mr. Heart did much to knit the proponents together. When word got out that opponents were seeking to oust Mr. Heart and that they had drafted a strong, critical letter, the proponents began to generate *support* for their pastor.

Attitudes Toward Conflict. Attitudes and ideas were significantly changed regarding the process of conflict itself. Proponents all agreed that they had learned much about the process of conflict. They learned that if the parish seeks to do its mission in the world it will experience conflict and controversy. Mr. Heart had always viewed reconciliation as the keystone to his ministry and conflict as a problem to overcome. Now he realizes that "the way to reconciliation is through conflict and forgiveness." As Mr. Heart described his experience: "I learned a great deal. I saw that conflict belongs within the framework of reconciliation and not outside it. I now see the primary thing is to be forthright. Let the tensions develop. Now I would talk about Alinsky, or anything else, on Palm Sunday." Other supporters of the Alinsky proposal also cited this lesson. As one exclaimed: "Conflict is a necessary part of parish life. A community such as ours can never resolve conflict completely. It is a process in which some real honest giving on both sides must take place."

A second lesson learned about conflict was that it need not be destructive. Opponents generally claimed that the experience was only destructive. Proponents, however, said the experience was both destructive and constructive. It was constructive since it enabled the church to make a significant breakthrough. Many persons were pushed through the apathy barrier and forced to think new thoughts and to decide on important issues. The explosion triggered by the Alinsky proposal definitely ended the drift that the church had experienced through the "years of disillusionment and decline" from 1962 to 1966. Although the proponents expressed sadness over being alienated from so many fellow members, they expressed confidence that the church was on the way to renewed vitality.

In addition to learning that conflict is a parish reality when the church takes its mission seriously and that conflict need not be destructive, church members learned of the important role of communication in resolving conflict. They all agreed that communication had broken down during the explosion and that in the future much more work had to be done to ensure good lines of communication within the congregation. They suggested that more small discussion groups on the order of PCE would be helpful. Also, they saw a need to bridge the informational, theological, and motivational gaps that exist between the local parish and the presbytery. With the exception of Mr. Rip, none of those who supported the Alinsky proposal knew anything at all about CORAR's program, and this fact disturbed them. So the members came to recognize the need for greater communication both within the congregation and with its presbytery.

Education. Substantive education definitely did occur at Fargo. Proponents said they were much better informed on problems of race and poverty in the Bay Area, the nature and purpose of community organization, and the man Saul Alinsky. Opponents claimed they learned a good deal about Alinsky, but, because of the emotional nature of the discussion, they didn't get much new information about race and poverty problems. It seems their primary interest was not the problems of the ghetto, but rather the problem of how to change the position of Fargo Church on the Alinsky proposal.

Opponents were convinced that they learned a great deal about Presbyterian polity and the political character of the San Francisco Presbytery. In their own words: "We learned the presbytery was controlled by a bunch of liberals who don't care about us out here." Surprisingly, no one in the Fargo Church continued to work with the Ad Hoc Appeals Committee to develop a strategy to counter the alleged liberal domination of presbytery.

It is difficult to say how the education affected people's decisions. Most people felt the attempts at education failed to change attitudes. No instance was reported of anyone who originally opposed or supported the issue changing his position. A dozen or so persons were known to have been at first uncommitted and then later decided to support the issue. There were also reports of "some persons" who were uncommitted in the beginning and then decided to oppose the proposal. Since most of the educational attempts took place after the community was polarized, it is understandable that they did not have much influence. Although new facts were learned about such things as race and poverty problems, polity, etc., the content of the educational process primarily served to reinforce feelings rather than to inform judgments.

Overall Impact on the Congregation. Members who remained with the church after the conflict felt that the experience had enabled them to break through the apathy and disillusionment that had kept the congregation bogged down from 1962 through 1966. That stage in the church's life has ended, but the big question now is whether the new era should be entitled "death" or "renewal"? Certainly if one takes only such indicators as budget, membership, and internal programs, the future of Fargo Church looks problematic. At the time of our study the church had already sold the parsonage to meet its financial obligations, and the session was discussing the possibility of selling additional church property. Mr. Rip saw little hope for the survival of a typical parish church, but he envisaged prospects if the congregation were willing to experiment. "I see it this way," he said. "CORAR has a problem—they need $200,000 in order to support Alinsky. Our church property is worth at least that; therefore, I suggest we sell our church and give the money to the presbytery for the support of Alinsky. Presbytery could carry out the sale. Then we could set up an organization here for the purpose of securing federal funds. We would use the money to build some low-income housing units. The congregation could use the meeting hall of the apartment building for its activities. Other parishes have done this kind of thing. I suggest this because as long as we move for justice in things like housing, the people of Fargo will not join us. I see little hope for a big community of servants there. This plan is a sacrifice aimed at creating a real serving community." What Mr. Rip is saying is that the maintenance of the local church can fail, while the mission of the church succeeds. In fact, he is saying that the maintenance function, as presently conceived, must fail, if the mission function is to succeed.

2. *For the Community*

Others in the congregation are looking in the same direction as Mr. Rip, although in less radical terms. Those favoring Alinsky firmly believe that although the church is suffering as an institution, its members have become more mature and dedicated Christians. They point out that stewardship pledges now come in on time and are paid in full. Especially is this new vitality evident, they say, in the church's commitment to social action. Indeed they maintain that for the first time Fargo Church is moving toward real involvement in sociopolitical affairs of the community. The signs of vitality pointed to are these:

a. The Confession of 1967 is taken seriously.
b. There is an acknowledged need for a quality adult education program with a direct focus on pressing social issues.
c. There is a renewed interest in liturgy and new forms of worship.
d. The church is one of the members of the Cooperative Parish, an effort of four Protestant denominations in Fargo to cooperate in planning and programming. This

cooperative effort began in the summer of 1966 as the
pastors and a few laymen from the congregation met to
discuss their common problems to seek solutions.

e. The church is in the newly formed Fargo Community
Organization. This is an organization made up of representatives from two open-housing groups, six churches,
the American Federation of Teachers, and the Ministerial
Association. The group is seeking "to cultivate a climate
for open housing and integration."

It is clear the congregation has broken through the barrier
that kept it from carrying out a vigorous social mission. But
without some institutional muscle behind this new zeal, it is
questionable whether the church's new thrust will have lasting significance. Prior to the Alinsky conflict the church had
the institutional resources for a strong community-centered
program, but the internal division of opinion paralyzed it. The
Alinsky conflict had the effect of reversing the situation. Now
that the church has reached a consensus on purposes and goals,
it lacks much of the institutional resources necessary for successful implementation. One hopeful sign is that the church
is aware of its dilemma and is taking steps to overcome its
plight. The development of the cooperative parish moves in
the direction of forming a strong institutional base.

7

Pleasant Ridge

Pleasant Ridge is a fairly new, small, and extremely wealthy church. Its history began on August 5, 1958, when Rev. Isaiah Logan was appointed organizing pastor for a new church development in the Pleasant Ridge–Lexington section of the East Bay. While surveying the area to determine potential church response, Dr. Logan met the Randolphs, a family who not only supported the idea but also offered their home as a meeting place.

Despite the wealth of the early members, the first phase of the congregation's life was marked by a genuine struggle for survival. Since no church building existed, it was necessary to lease the Pleasant Ridge Public School. Thirty persons attended the first worship service held in the school building on November 30, 1958. From that time until the completion of the church building in 1965, it was necessary for a committee to set up chairs for each worship service and then dismantle the "sanctuary" after the service. Despite these provisional arrangements, the congregation grew. In 1959, fifty-three persons petitioned the presbytery to organize them into a church to be called the Pleasant Ridge United Presbyterian Church. Dr. Logan was unanimously called as the permanent pastor. The

congregation grew rapidly, and already by 1960 the membership had reached 150.

At that point, however, recruitment subsided and for a
while there was substantial doubt whether the congregation
would continue to exist. The institutional impetus that united
the church during this period was the $260,000 building cam-
paign for the proposed church plant. This building campaign
revitalized the charter members and, in fact, gave rise to a
renewed growth period that brought membership to the
present number of 325.

The church building itself is symbolic of the nature of the
congregation. An impressive A-frame structure, the sanctuary
opens behind the altar into a floor-to-ceiling plate-glass win-
dow which overlooks the gothic beauty of a pine grove. The
fact that worship takes place in these spectacular surround-
ings has made the sanctuary an ideal place for marriages and
a religious shrine for Pleasant Ridge–Lexington residents. Located at the edge of a serene valley village, the church seems,
in its very being, to symbolize peace.

Peace may very well be the keynote in the life of the Pleasant
Ridge congregation. In our interview with Dr. Ernest Comfort,
the interim pastor at the time of the Alinsky proposal, his first
words were these: "To understand the congregation you have
to know that these people moved to Pleasant Ridge to find
quiet. They are an extremely wealthy and successful group
who want to rest after the hectic pace of days at the office.
They came to suburbia in order not to be bothered, and
you're in the wrong place if you're looking for active demon-
strators for social reform."

CHARACTERISTICS OF THE CONGREGATION

Socioeconomic Characteristics. Of our six congregations,
Pleasant Ridge is the wealthiest. Its membership consists exclusively of upper- and upper-middle-class families. Average

income is estimated at $20,000 per family. Members are extremely well educated; advanced college degrees are the general rule rather than the exception. Occupations cluster in the scientific, technical, business, and professional categories. As indicators of the life-style of the members, two facts may be mentioned: first, there is a zoning ordinance that requires that every family own an "estate" of at least three acres; second, one of the principal forms of recreation on the Ridge is horseback riding, and nearly every family owns at least one riding horse. Pleasant Ridge seems to epitomize the often-discussed "affluence" of today's suburban America. Both the church and the community are ultraconservative politically, but there is no evidence that any of the Pleasant Ridge members are John Birchers.

Theological Orientation. Generally speaking, Pleasant Ridge members are theologically conservative. This is due not simply to the conservative nature of the community but also to the central role played by Dr. Logan in membership recruitment. Dr. Logan's personality, preaching style, and conservative theology alienated potential members who were interested in a socially active and liberal church. At present no more than five members could be called activists.

Probably a majority of the congregation are within what we have called the "Churchly Christianity" camp. This group is represented in its extreme form by a small number of fundamentalists who feel that the church should focus exclusively on worship, prayer, and Bible study. Seven or eight families, for example, regularly attend Sunday evening services at a nearby Pentecostal church. Strong support for a pietistic position is given by a group of members who live in Shady Pines, a nearby home for the aged. Even among the more moderate wing of the congregation, pietist tendencies exist, and the concept of mission is limited. The general understanding of mission is that the church should witness to the "unchurched millionaires" of the Pleasant Ridge–Lexington community and bring them to Christ. Very little emphasis is given to problems beyond the confines of the Ridge.

There can be no doubt that the congregation is overwhelmingly opposed to corporate church involvement in social and political matters. In Dr. Comfort's words, "We don't accept the church's floating off into a parade." With few exceptions the members feel that the church's task is to focus on spiritual matters, to talk about Christ and the Bible, and to make *individuals* more Christian. These attitudes were revealed in answers to five questions. Eight of our ten informants stated that, when a community faces a problem, it is better for the church to respond through its individual members than as a body. When we asked our informants whether it is more important to change individuals or society, four chose changing individuals, five chose "both," but felt that society could only be changed by changing individuals, and one offered no opinion. Again, eight of our ten informants gave negative responses to the question whether the church should take stands on social and political issues. As one representative member put it, "No, the pastor tells me about Christ and the Bible; *I* take the stands." In response to our question whether the pastor should be directly involved in community affairs, six members said no and only two said yes. The pastor, it was felt, should focus on his own flock and avoid speaking out. Finally, as Pleasant Ridge members see it, the role of the church in relation to secular society is to make individuals more Christian by preaching the gospel and witnessing to Christ.

Pastoral Leadership. For purposes of coping with the trend toward increased social action and involvement, Pleasant Ridge has had almost no pastoral leadership. Dr. Logan had leadership ability, as evidenced by his success in building the new church. His belief, however, was that the pastor is only qualified to lead on purely ethical and theological matters. Under Dr. Logan's pastorate, the church's program focused on

worship, recruitment, and building. There was no noteworthy
adult education at all. This situation was heightened when
Dr. Logan retired in late 1965 and Dr. Comfort was called as
interim pastor. Dr. Comfort is a political and theological conservative who feels that the pastor's principal role is to "teach
the Bible" and develop the Christian character of his members. More significantly, however, he felt that an interim pastor
should not embark on any dramatic new programs or policies.

Thus, thoughout its history and particularly during the
Alinsky crisis, Pleasant Ridge had pastors who reinforced the
predominant tendency toward political conservatism and
theological pietism. No effort was made to keep the congregation informed about the changing shape of the church at
large. The new pastor who has replaced Dr. Comfort is expected to provide more liberal leadership than his predeces-
sors, but his pastorate began only after the events with which
we are concerned.

Past Experience. We have previously suggested that "peace"
may be the word which most accurately describes the Pleasant
Ridge–Lexington community and the Pleasant Ridge Church.
This is certainly the case as far as past experience with conflict is concerned. In order to provide a comparative basis for
evaluating the decision-making process on the Alinsky matter
we asked all our informants to describe the most intense conflict that the congregation had faced prior to 1966. Without a
single exception, the Pleasant Ridge members stated that apart
from the Alinsky proposal there has not been a single emotionally charged conflict in the congregation's history. One family
withdrew because it felt that the Sunday school building
should have been constructed before the sanctuary. An incipient debate over giving funds for the Selma demonstrations was
resolved quietly by a negative vote of the session. Proposition
14 caused some excitement, particularly because several session members advocated a corporate stand in favor of open
housing. The consensus, however, is that the discussion never
gave rise to a real conflict. The session handled the matter by

issuing a moderate "statement of principles" and by remind-
ing the pastor that he should concentrate on preaching the
Bible. Despite a growing restiveness concerning the attitude
of the church at large on social action, Dr. Comfort was able
to characterize the congregation as "very placid." As he put it,
"I never heard a heated word."

Based on the absence of experience with conflict and the
conservative bias of the members, a likely hypothesis would
have been that the members would emphatically oppose conflict within the church. Yet to our surprise among our clearly
conservative informants only one felt that conflict is a sign
that something is wrong. Two considered it to be a necessary
evil. The other two, together with the two liberals, saw conflict as a positive sign. Thus, although there is some emphasis
on "peace and harmony," there is also substantial verbal
acknowledgment of the need to air all sides of issues openly.
Our two liberal informants, however, expressed the opinion
that the church does, in fact, shy away from conflict and that
there is no forum within the church for airing differences of
opinion.

What has been the past experience in attitude toward race
and poverty problems among members of Pleasant Ridge?
Increasingly the members have come to see that the country
is facing a real problem in these areas and that the church
should do "something" about it. Their feeling, by and large,
is that the church should respond by creating an awareness of
the problem and by emphasizing the gospel message of concern and responsibility for our brothers. Although Dr. Comfort feels that he has never known such a concerned group,
many individual members seemed to think that actual involvement has been at an embarrassing minimum. The main
focus of concern for the Pleasant Ridge people is a ghetto
in nearby Lexington. Activity in the ghetto, before 1966, had
been primarily on an individual basis, with church involvement limited to providing monetary support for a mission
house and a summer festival. Much of the individual concern

has been expressed through such traditional channels as visiting jails and hospitals, sewing, teaching crafts, and donating food. The members did not feel that the ghettos in Oakland and San Francisco were "their problem."

Structural Elements. The congregation is unusually homogeneous. It is controlled by one leadership elite (roughly twenty-five individuals) that has the backing of nearly all the more inactive members. Control of the session and rapport with the pastors has allowed this elite to direct the process of decision-making with relative ease. The only "opposition" to these leaders consists of not more than five activists who have relatively little voice in church decisions. This latter group is prominent in the Church and Society Committee, but one of its members, the chairman of that committee, feels that the activists exist in relative isolation and with a minimum of interaction and communication with the governing leaders. The leadership elite of the congregation, in turn, has tended to run its own show, paying very little attention to developments in other churches and in the presbytery at large.

DYNAMICS OF DECISION-MAKING

When the news broke concerning the proposal to finance Saul Alinsky, Pleasant Ridge faced the first major emotionally charged issue in its history. Our informants were unanimous in characterizing the response of the congregation as "extremely intense." Certainly, at the very least, the issue provoked more discussion and emotion than any other in the history of Pleasant Ridge. The CORAR motion was opposed by 98 to 99 percent of the membership, and the number of individuals favoring Alinsky was definitely not more than five. Dr. Comfort recalls having received more than fifty phone calls concerning the issue and having had at least ten or twelve personal appointments. It soon became apparent that the "enemy" was presbytery and that the conflict was not an in-group matter. A very typical response seems to have been the threat to with-draw pledges from all Presbyterian activities.

Despite the extraordinary intensity of the controversy, only "normally authorized" processes of internal decision-making were employed. The first notice of the proposed action came with CORAR's official call. Mrs. Randolph, the appointed presbytery delegate, sensed the importance of the meeting and suggested to Dr. Comfort that Mr. Ralph Davis represent the church instead. Davis, a lawyer, was the acknowledged expert on Alinsky. Mrs. Randolph felt that he would have a better chance of being heard on the floor of presbytery. The session considered the matter on April 11. Each member was requested to state his position on the matter, and since only one favored Alinsky, the following action was implemented: a vote was taken which confirmed that the session opposed the motion, Mr. Davis was elected as alternative delegate, and the delegates were instructed to vote against the motion.

In the aftermath of April 12, the session considered the Alinsky issue in at least three additional meetings. The session appointed a special fact-finding committee which did extensive research and reported back to the regular meetings. During the meetings, the session split into factions, and the discussion became fairly "acrimonious." For the first time in the church's history, parliamentary maneuvering was used in a session meeting. The outcome of these deliberations was a formal decision by the session to go on record as opposing the action. A statement was drafted declaring opposition, appealing the decision and requesting reconsideration and this statement was mailed to presbytery headquarters.

The decision-making process was handled almost entirely by the session. This is a perfectly normal procedure. At Pleas-ant Ridge, congregational meetings are held once a year and at such other times as the session decides. In this case, the session decided that since the church was 99 percent in agree-ment, nothing would be gained by convening the entire congregation. Their feeling was that open discussion of the issue would unnecessarily outrage the members. The matter was, however, communicated to the entire congregation through two channels: a bulletin announcement and a statement by Mr. Davis during a Sunday morning service.

Viewing the matter in retrospect, we feel justified in saying that the keynote of the decision-making process was preserving tranquillity and suppressing conflict. Dr. Comfort has stated that his guiding intention throughout the spring was to "avoid the furor and keep it calm." Thus, he acted as "moderator" of the session discussions and maintained official neutrality. It was well known, however, that he was bitterly opposed to CORAR's action and operating behind the scenes, through the Ad Hoc Appeals Committee and other channels, to see that the action was rescinded. It is not difficult to appraise the results of Dr. Comfort's decision. There can be no doubt that the situation was a difficult one, namely, to be an interim pastor at a time when a very young and inexperienced congregation faced its first controversy. Nevertheless, his silence did have an extremely profound effect: it left a total vacuum in the area of interpreting the presbytery's action to the outraged congregation. Thus, although the decision was announced to the entire congregation, no effort was made to explain the reasons behind CORAR's action. This left the congregation with unmitigated anger and bitterness toward CORAR. Furthermore, it prevented any real encounter with the need for some kind of action on race and poverty and the importance of formulating more acceptable alternatives. In short, because of the lack of interpretation, no real dialogue with CORAR was begun, and the anger remained destructive rather than constructive.

How did the Pleasant Ridge members define the situation that had been thrust upon them? Four principal issues were discussed during the days after April 12. First and foremost was Saul Alinsky. Specific arguments against Alinsky will be discussed below; at this point it suffices to say that nearly all the members felt a strong antipathy toward the man. Second was the question of corporate church involvement. The Alinsky proposal surfaced in full force the latent anger that had been developing for years on this issue. It became one of the major substantive issues in the controversy. A third major issue was, from the members' viewpoint, the business insanity of giving away $200,000 without any strings attached; that is, without any provision for supervision or direction concerning the use of funds. Whereas in other congregations this matter tended to be of only peripheral interest, in Pleasant Ridge it was a predominant focus of attention, particularly among the most informed and concerned members. The fourth factor— in reality a source of anger rather than a substantive issue— was the abusive treatment which the members felt they received from CORAR. As we hypothesized, there was real resentment over what seemed to be a lack of adequate preparation. More significant, however, was the anger of the congregation concerning the treatment of Mr. Davis at the April 12 meeting. After having prepared an extensive statement, Mr. Davis was cut off in the middle of his remarks in a way that Dr. Comfort described as "disgusting, filthy."

Let us take a closer look at the content of the discussion within the congregation. At the session level, the principal issue was the absurdity, from a business standpoint, of granting $200,000 to an unpredictable man with no strings attached. Within the congregation at large, however, the focus was Saul Alinsky. In view of the official decision to refrain from formal discussions, informal conversation became the main channel through which most members aired their grievances. The principal objections raised in these informal discussions concerned Alinsky's not being a Christian, his "gangster" tactics, and his personal offensiveness.

For most members, Alinsky's religious position alone was enough to disqualify him. In addition to the simple fact that Alinsky is not a Christian, members were offended by his "not even being a good Jew," by his apparent pride in his agnostic philosophy, and by his tendency to make disparaging remarks about the WASP churchmen. Since Alinsky is non-Christian, it was felt, he cannot be relied upon to pursue Christian goals. Furthermore, the opinion was voiced that if there is not a single Christian who can handle the task, then "we should quit." The second most significant argument against Alinsky focused on his use of non-Christian or "gangster" tactics. This objection was based on theological, not practical, grounds. Members of Pleasant Ridge Church feel strongly that Christ taught us to love our fellowman and that social action based on exacerbating and channeling hatred is inconsistent with Christianity's ethical teachings. Third in importance was the objection to Alinsky's personal style, particularly his profanity. Our informants frequently referred to Alinsky as a "vile person" and cited the diaper and fart-in incidents. (This refers to an alleged protest plan announced by Alinsky to feed beans to a large number of people and then have them attend a symphony concert performance.)

In addition to these three central objections, a number of others were raised. Alinsky's apparent intention to destroy the social order was repugnant to several informants. There was a general skepticism about the effectiveness of Alinsky's method based primarily on the assumption that it would create new and antagonistic power blocs. Frequent references were also made to Alinsky's wealth, specifically his "mansion" in Carmel, and the inference was drawn that he is using the poor for his own monetary ends. Finally, there was a feeling that the Oakland people did not want Alinsky, and that their rejection of him was well-founded since, in reality, he "tries to create rather than assuage a sense of segregation."

The discussion focused so completely on Alinsky *the man* that almost no attention was given to the strengths and weaknesses of mass community organization per se, to the needs and plight of the ghetto, or to the question of alternative proposals. Overwhelming attention to questions of means obscured the issue of ends to be sought.

Determining the extent of membership involvement in this matter is a delicate task. Doubtless, the controversy was the most intense issue in the history of Pleasant Ridge Church. Yet deep involvement was mainly limited to those on the session. Only twenty-five to forty members of the congregation actually attended the presbytery meetings, the educational meetings held by CORAR, or the Ad Hoc Appeals Committee meetings. In terms of subjective or emotional involvement, on the other hand, the percentages are much higher. At least half of the members felt they had been "deeply involved," and it was generally acknowledged that nearly everyone in the congregation was at least moderately involved and excited.

CONSEQUENCES

1. *For the Church*

Measurable Effects. The "non-decision" of June 7 had the expected repercussions within Pleasant Ridge Church. Despite the clear language of the bipartisan committee's report leaving the door open for a later invitation to Alinsky, the Pleasant Ridge members interpreted the vote as a defeat for CORAR. Thus, the members did not feel impelled to carry out their threats to withdraw funds or membership. For this reason, the quantifiable effects of the controversy were minimal. No families withdrew from membership in Pleasant Ridge. There was no measurable budget loss attributable to Alinsky. Although Dr. Comfort stated that giving to the Fifty Million Fund was cut to a tenth of what it would have been, this opinion has not been verified. The nearly unanimous feeling of our informants, however, was that a catastrophe had been narrowly averted: if Alinsky had been asked, massive retaliation might have been expected.

Relationships Within the Church. The Alinsky controversy had very little effect on the interaction among members of the Pleasant Ridge congregation. There were no evident cases of alienation of existing friendships. Only a few cases of newly

discovered or stronger relationships formed. Only one informant claimed to have gained greater respect toward those
within the congregation who disagreed with him. Whether the
controversy created an increased hostility toward those in disagreement is somewhat ambiguous. In Dr. Comfort's opinion,
at least one of the local members favoring the CORAR motion
came under a noticeable amount of criticism and perhaps some
degree of ostracism. And at least one of our informants acknowledged an "increased suspicion" toward his adversaries.
On the whole, however, the internal relations of the congregation seem to have weathered the storm.

The effect of the controversy on relationships with Presbyterians in other congregations and in staff positions was more
pronounced. To some degree, the controversy brought the
Pleasant Ridge members into contact with members of other
churches. The chief avenue of contact was the Ad Hoc Appeals Committee activities and the CORAR area meetings. We
have estimated that twenty-five to forty members participated
in events sponsored by these two groups. However, no significant or lasting group or individual relationships arose from
this participation. Only two Pleasant Ridge members, for example, actually joined the Ad Hoc group. The effect of the
Alinsky controversy on attitudes toward official church bodies,
however, was substantial. Those who professed knowledge
about CORAR felt that the Commission was irresponsible and
viewed it with suspicion and distrust. They felt that staff leaders were gullible and showed bad judgment. Finally, there was
a general loss of confidence in the Presbyterian Church. Despite these reservations, half of our informants felt that the
experience had made it easier to understand and work with
those who see things differently. Thus, the seeds of redemption
may have been planted amid the acres of discouragement.

Attitudes Toward Conflict. Very little seems to have been
accomplished within the Pleasant Ridge congregation relative
to education in the realities of conflict. This, of course, stems
in part from the effort to suppress conflict and discussion in

this instance rather than confront it and learn from it. Also, since the congregation was nearly unanimous in its opposition to the proposal, the anger was mainly directed toward external "enemies," and the congregation was not forced to develop any new tools for handling in-group conflict. On the other hand, the members did come to realize that to whatever degree they chose to participate in *presbytery* decision-making, they would be thrust into controversial areas. Despite this development, our informants were convinced that this particular controversy did very little to help the congregation accept conflict as a reality of parish life. There is no evidence of any new sense of openness. There is some feeling, however, that the conservatives are being taught a lesson over the long haul that the church cannot remain silent and avoid conflict.

Education. Substantive education on race and poverty problems was not as extensive as we had anticipated. Several of the key leaders of the church, including Dr. Comfort, stated that no major attempt was made to educate the congregation. Rather, the principal goal was to calm tensions and suppress conflict. This program certainly had the effect of minimizing the amount of education that took place. In fact, most of our informants stated that "no education" took place on poverty problems or community organization. One member even opined that the effect was negative in the sense that sympathetic individuals were alienated from the civil rights struggle by the Alinsky dispute. Dr. Comfort, Mrs. Randolph, and Mr. Davis, however, are of the opinion that some education did take place. It seems certain, in any case, that minimal education took place on the issue of community organization and that whatever education was gained about Alinsky did very little to change anyone's prior opinion.

There is one matter upon which it is felt that substantial education did take place. This education may be summed up in the following quotation which represents the position of five of our informants: "We had our eyes opened about how the Church is being run, and we're not going to sit back and allow it to happen any more." What the Pleasant Ridge laity came to feel was that the church is being led by a group of clergy and staff who do not in any sense represent the feelings of the majority of the laity. The reason that these men have been able to take charge of the machinery is that the laity have abdicated their responsibility and concern. With responsible lay participation at a minimum, the liberals and activists have taken over by default and are leading the church "down the primrose path." Several of the influential Pleasant Ridge lay leaders indicated a determination to put a stop to this situation. Their position was roughly, "From now on we're going to make sure that we attend all the meetings and keep them from getting away with anything." To some degree, there has been an attempt to institutionalize this plan through two channels: the remnant of the Ad Hoc Appeals Committee and the Presbyterian Lay Committee. Jumping somewhat beyond our data, we would hypothesize that the Alinsky matter may have provided a substantial impetus and entering wedge for the efforts of the Presbyterian Lay Committee in this part of the country.

Overall Impact on the Congregation. The Alinsky controversy certainly did not give rise to any renewal or revitalization of Pleasant Ridge's parish life. If anything, it may have produced a slight deterioration. In Dr. Comfort's opinion, the harm done was "1,000 times greater than the good that came from education." As an overall appraisal, the members of Pleasant Ridge feel that the experience was destructive except for the single fact that it opened their eyes concerning what was happening within the church at large. After the June 7 non-decision, the emotion level returned nearly to normal. Nevertheless, the members watch every new move by Alinsky with concern and they feel that if he does ally himself with the church, the entire outrage will be repeated. Indeed, one informant predicted that the church would lose 95 percent of its members. This appears to be a threat which was exaggerated for political purposes. Nevertheless, even the calmer and more realistic members fear that "bringing Alinsky in the back door" would cause the withdrawal of at least twenty wealthy families and would create a substantial threat to the continued existence of the church. Generally, the experience has created a feeling of suspicion and distrust among the members of Pleasant Ridge. In Dr. Comfort's opinion: "The presbytery is in terrible shape. It's pathetic. I've never seen anything like it before. There is a fierce animosity."

2. For the Community

We have stated that the Alinsky controversy did not substantially change the attitudes of Pleasant Ridge members toward race and poverty problems. The discussion focused so heavily on Alinsky's personality and the internal problems of the Presbyterian Church that it did not provide the bulk of the congregation with any new exposure to the ghetto situation. Leaders who were more deeply involved did get some new insights, but these were counterbalanced by an increase in anger and a sense of alienation from the civil rights cause. Only two of our informants claimed increased sympathy for the Negro plight.

The question remains whether the discussion within the Pleasant Ridge congregation had any spin-off effects for other church programs. The answer to this question is yes, but the extent of the spin-off is slight. Progress is acknowledged in several channels: a more active Church and Society Committee, discussions about increased efforts in the Lexington ghetto, and perhaps some rise in support for less objectionable race and poverty programs. The other significant by-product may be an increased affiliation with conservative lay groups. Some informants believe that the Alinsky controversy has led to conservative decisions by pulpit committees which will seek to replace liberals by hiring conservative pastors. However, this last spin-off did not occur in Pleasant Ridge, where the new pastor, while definitely not an angry young man, is also not on the political and theological right fringe.

8

Interpretation of Congregational Responses: The Schizophrenic Church

This chapter seeks to lift up important findings from the congregational case studies. Since it was necessary to cut seventy-five pages from our original manuscript, the case study of Park Street and of Evangelical have been omitted. Each represents highly committed positions of pro and con. Since conflict was external rather than internal, we have not detailed the internal dynamics in Part Two, but we do report their overall responses in this chapter. The omitted material is on file with Project CLEAR. In analyzing information from presbytery leaders in Chapter 3, we formulated certain hypotheses to be elaborated more fully by the congregational data. The conclusions were: (1) that the church has a substantive and structural dualism; (2) that the Alinsky controversy brought the dualism to the surface and sharply polarized the presbytery; (3) that the procedures for conflict resolution broke down under the strain and produced a "non-decision"; and (4) that the results of the entire effort were highly ambiguous. In the course of the discussion, we suggested the following hypotheses: (1) that there would be a "gap" between the attitudes of the presbytery leaders and the majority of local members; (2) that the congregation studies would indicate severe polarization; (3) that there would be a similar procedural breakdown; and (4) that the results would be similarly ambiguous. On the other hand, we predicted positive findings in education on substantive matters, education on conflict, and spin-off benefits for the community. Do the congregational studies confirm or disprove these conclusions and hypotheses?

In the first place, the suggested "gap" or structural dualism was supported by the congregational data. What we suspected was that the liberal wing of the church, comprising a small majority of clergymen and a minority of laymen, had institutionalized itself in such a way that it could press for action programs more radical than the great bulk of laymen could accept. In other words, there seemed to be a gap between the leaders and the constituency. Thus, despite the fact that the presbytery delegates originally passed the Alinsky proposal 107–88, we expected to find that the proposal did not command a similar majority among Presbyterian churchmen generally.

We have reasonable grounds for feeling that our hypothesis has been confirmed. In the first place, we attempted to choose six churches that would represent an even division across the spectrum of support and dissent. Based on opinions expressed by presbytery leaders, we expected Pleasant Ridge and Evangelical to be strongly opposed to Alinsky, Westminster and Fargo to be divided, and Christ Church and Park Street to be strongly in favor. The disparity between what we expected and what we found is reflected in the following table:

TABLE 1. ATTITUDE TOWARD ALINSKY—% PRO/CON

Church	Expected		Actual	
Pleasant Ridge	10/90	Against	1/99	Against
Evangelical	10/90		1/99	
Westminster	30/70	Split	10/90	Split
Fargo	50/50		40/60	
Christ Church	80/20	For	65/35	For
Park Street	95/ 5		95/ 5	

In only one case (Park Street) were the Alinsky supporters as numerous as we expected. The unexpected strength of the opposition to Alinsky is clear from the following facts: the overwhelming (99–1) opposition in Pleasant Ridge and Evangelical; the very strong opposition in Westminster, which we had assumed to be moderate; the split in Christ Church, which we had assumed to be strongly in favor; and the small number of members in Park Street, the only strongly supportive congregation. As the following table illustrates, the approximate numerical breakdown of opposition and support in our six congregations was roughly:

TABLE 2. ATTITUDE TOWARD ALINSKY—NUMBER PRO/CON

Church	Pro	Con
Pleasant Ridge	5	320
Evangelical	1	999
Westminster	250	2,350
Fargo	180	270
Christ Church	780	420
Park Street	70	5
Total	1,286	4,364

Based on these estimates, we may conclude that the hypothesized gap between leaders and laymen is a reality. The 107–88 presbytery vote favoring Alinsky must be seen as evidence of the extent of the gap rather than a true indication of the general attitudes of churchmen. The institutionalized liberal position does not reflect the position of the laity.

By now, it is clear that the Alinsky proposal brought this underlying split to the surface with explosive force. As the table on the opposite page shows, four of our six congregations had highly intense responses.

Obviously there was no reason for Park Street to have an explosion, since its members nearly unanimously agreed with the April 12 decision. Why the 35 percent opposition in Christ

TABLE 3. INTENSITY OF CONGREGATIONAL RESPONSE

Church	Most Intense	Very Intense	Moderately Intense	Calm
Pleasant Ridge	X			
Evangelical	X			
Westminster		X		
Fargo	X			
Christ Church			X	
Park Street				X

Church did not explode will be discussed extensively below. Furthermore, we shall have to explain why Westminster with a 10–90 split had lower intensity than Pleasant Ridge (1–99) and Evangelical (1–99), on the one hand, and Fargo (40–60), on the other. In any case, the proposal incited explosively angry responses from the numerically preponderant opposition.

This led, as we predicted, to a severe polarization. With the sole exception of Christ Church, the controversy seems to have had a divisive effect on relations within the presbytery. Pleasant Ridge, with its strongly conservative bias, developed a strong sense of alienation from the church at large. Within its own ranks, Pleasant Ridge experienced some feelings of increased cohesion in the face of an external enemy, but this was offset by a growing feeling that the time to leave the church may be near. At Evangelical, the divisive tendencies were so pronounced that sentiment began to favor an actual withdrawal of the congregation from presbytery. At Fargo, the divisiveness focused mainly on internal relations and eventuated in the loss of seventy members. Similarly, Westminster experienced both anger with the church at large and an internal split between the newly consolidated moderate wing and the increasingly hostile conservatives. Although Alinsky was not the sole cause of the split, the consideration of alternatives for racial action was part of the general trend. Finally, at Park Street, we sensed a growing alienation from the church at large springing from the recognition of the intransient power

of the conservatives. Perhaps the overall effect of the debate
will be clearer if we summarize these comments in the following sketch.

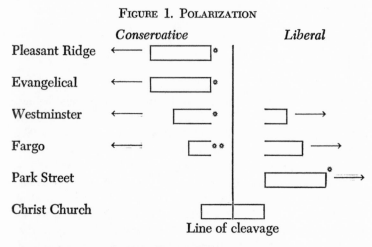

FIGURE 1. POLARIZATION

* Increased alienation from church at large.
** Left the church.

How did the congregations attempt to cope with polarization?
At the presbytery level we suggested that the machinery broke
down and eventuated in a "non-decision." Things were not
substantially better at the local congregation level. The first
procedural matter which we tried to pin down was the degree
to which the congregations were able to keep their attention
focused on the substantive issues presented by the CORAR
proposal. The following is a summary table indicating the
nature of the issues that were most important in each church.

At Pleasant Ridge, Evangelical, and Fargo, the debate got
sidetracked on nonsubstantive issues and was never able to
return. Westminster, despite its heavy opposition, appears to
have had better results. Park Street had relatively good issue
focus. Finally, Christ Church did astonishingly well consider-

TABLE 4. ISSUE FOCUS

Church	Rating	1a	1b	1c	1d	1e	1f	2a	2b	2c	2d
Park St.	Not				×			×		×	×
	Not very								×		×
	Moderate		×	×		×	×				
	Very										
Christ Church	Not							×		×	×
	Not very				×			×	×		
	Moderate		×			×	×				
	Very	×									
Fargo	Not		×	×	×		×				
	Not very		×								
	Moderate					×		×	×		
	Very									×	×
Westminster	Not						×				
	Not very									×	×
	Moderate		×	×		×		×	×		
	Very				×	×					
Evangelical	Not						×			|	
	Not very		×		×					|	
	Moderate		×			×		×		|	
	Very				×				×	|	×
Pleasant Ridge	Not				×	×				|	
	Not very		×							|	×
	Moderate		×			×	×			|	
	Very							×	×	|	

Issues

1. Substantive
  a. Alinsky's Methods and Past Performance
  b. Efficacy of Community Organization
  c. Alternatives to Community Organization
  d. Nature of Social Problem
  e. Church and Social Action
  f. Business risks

2. Nonsubstantive
  a. Alinsky's Personality
  b. CORAR's Tactics
  c. Tactics of Opposition within Congregation
  d. Countertactics

Rating on 1-5 scale
Pleasant Ridge 2
Evangelical 2
Westminster 3
Fargo 1
Christ Church 5
Park Street 4

150   THE SCHIZOPHRENIC CHURCH

ing its 35 percent opposition. In short, three of the congregations allowed the discussion to veer off course, while the other three kept their attention relatively centered on the substantive issues presented.

The second standard that we attempted to bring to bear on the processes of decision-making was the amount of communication between opposing camps. In this regard, the findings were not encouraging:

TABLE 5. COMMUNICATION AMONG OPPONENTS

Church	Ingroup			Outgroup		
	Good	Fair	Poor	Good	Fair	Poor
Pleasant Ridge			X			X
Evangelical	—	—	—			X
Westminster		X			X	
Fargo		X*				X
Christ Church	X				X	
Park Street		X				X

* Too little, after too many years of silence.

This poverty of communication across lines of loyalty occurred despite the CORAR area meetings and the Ad Hoc breakfast meetings. The uniform reaction of our informants from all six congregations was that the proceedings presented by their favorite group were fair and honest, whereas those of the opposition were biased and propagandistic. There is very little evidence that either set of meetings changed many people's minds. Furthermore, the conservative leaders strongly decried CORAR's refusal to communicate with them.

In addition to the spotty issue-focus and the breakdown of communication, a third finding seems to provide insight into the processes of decision-making, namely, their stereotyped and unimaginative nature. We have argued above that this debate was extremely intense and explosive throughout most of the presbytery. Thus, for example, three of our six congregations view it as the most intense ever and a fourth considers it to have been one of the most intense. Yet despite this fact, *not one* of the six congregations used anything other than "normal and authorized" procedures for dealing with it. There was *no experimentation* with new channels. The entire matter was handled through traditional procedures. Only Park Street and Christ Church, the two congregations least threatened by the proposal, had even begun to develop new methods and structures for handling hot issues. In short, on the basis of the relative inadequacy of issue-focus, and communication, and the unimaginative nature of the response, we are prepared to argue that the procedures for handling the conflict were as inadequate within the congregations as they were in the presbytery at large.

Thus far we have seen that the themes of gap, polarization, and inadequacy of process are reflected both in the presbytery and the congregations. Can the same be said about the crucial category of "non-decision"? On the face of it, the answer would seem to be negative. Four of the six congregations reached a clear decision on the Alinsky matter (Pleasant Ridge, Evangelical, and Westminster were against, while Park Street was in favor). Fargo and Christ Church considered the issue to be within the jurisdiction of the presbytery, not the local congregation. In an important but less obvious way, however, the "non-decision" of June 7 was a non-decision for the congregations as well. What happened on and after June 7 was that everyone believed what he wanted about the report and decision. For example, despite the strong endorsement of mass community organization and the statement that Alinsky was "in a class by himself," the report was taken by conservatives at Pleasant Ridge, Evangelical, and Westminster churches to mean that Alinsky would not be asked. Similarly, the liberals at Park Street, Fargo, and Christ Church assumed that the decision was to support Alinsky as soon as the ghettos asked for him. Clearly there was no meeting of minds and no genuine resolution of conflict. On the contrary, the conservatives stated time and again that the only reason they did not carry out their threats to leave the church was that Alinsky did not come. If, on the other hand, the church were to tie in with Alinsky at a later time, they predicted that the entire outrage would be repeated. At the same time, the liberals at Fargo and Christ Church were forming organizations and plans to get Alinsky under the call provision.

Gap, polarization, and non-decision at the presbytery level left us in doubt about the overall results of the Alinsky debate for the local congregations and the community. What has been learned in this regard from our case studies?

Perhaps the most positive hypothesis formulated before beginning the congregational studies was that the Alinsky debate gave rise to a substantial amount of education. This hypothesis was based on numerous assertions by presbytery leaders that the period of April to June, 1966, witnessed more education than any other period in the history of the presbytery. Furthermore, we expected that the education would focus on three different areas: race and poverty problems, the church and conflict, and church polity. Let us examine each of these areas.

To what degree did the discussion yield substantive education on race and poverty problems? Although education doubtless took place, our overall appraisal was that the amount was surprisingly and disappointingly small. At two of our congregations, Pleasant Ridge and Fargo, very little education occurred, since the former systematically avoided discussing the matter, and both parishes lost control of the discussion, which ended up in *ad hominem* squabbles rather than issue-centered debate. At the other four congregations "moderate" education took place. Evangelical and Westminster profited from their attempts to generate alternative programs, but the education did not reach very deeply into the membership. Finally, Christ Church and Park Street learned more about how to carry forward some of the directions which they had already established. Finally, one development raised skepticism about the amount of education that occurred. Despite the fact that "mass community organization" was the central tactical question involved, and despite numerous allegations that much had been learned about it, our informants rarely had any clear idea what it meant. Apart from the members of Park Street and a few experts elsewhere, it was obvious that "community organization" means nothing more than agencies cooperating in the community. The fundamental point concerning the development of an indigenous power bloc seems to have been missed.

Our second hypothesis was that the debate would produce greater tolerance for conflict within the church and more astute understanding of how to deal with it. This was based on a number of informants claiming that the church had become more "open" and "honest" as a result of having faced the Alinsky issue. Unfortunately, there was no easy way to test this hypothesis. Since we did not have reliable "before and after" data, we had to rely on after-the-fact judgments. In this regard, a large majority stated that no change had occurred and that the members had not been induced to accept conflict as a reality of parish life. Since no new methods for dealing with conflict were generated, it was not surprising that we found little evidence of increased astuteness in facing conflict.

In the area of our third hypothesis we discovered interesting results, but their overall effect was not what we had expected. Important education did take place concerning "Presbyterian polity." Once again, this education did not reach many members, but its impact may prove significant. The substance of the education—what the members learned—was how their opposition operated within the presbytery and how "we" would have to organize and act to meet that opposition to ensure that the church will do what "we" want.

The situation may be clarified by comparing the responses of our most liberal and conservative congregations, Park Street and Pleasant Ridge. Both congregations were nearly unanimous in their stand on CORAR's proposal. Consequently, the conflict tended to be with persons outside the congregation.

In both cases, communication with the opposition was not very great, and efforts to interpret and explain the opposition position were minimal. Our informants from both congregations were mainly skeptical about the amount of education that had taken place on race problems and on conflict management. In both cases, however, our informants made statements as follows: "We had our eyes opened as to the way the presbytery is run, and we have a clearer idea now about how to make sure that the church does the right thing." For the members of Pleasant Ridge, this meant the discovery that the conservatives had abdicated their responsibility and allowed the liberals to take over by default. The result was a determination to put a stop to the trend by organizing and activating the conservative laity. The chief vehicle for such a mobilization was to be the Presbyterian Lay Committee. At Park Street, on the other hand, the members discovered both the strength of the conservative opposition and the difficulty of mobilizing social action. They also realized, however, that a "black face on the floor of presbytery" could have substantial impact and that success would require astute planning and organization.

In short, the Alinsky controversy gave rise to a surprising amount of education on polity and politics. The effect of this education, however, was to exacerbate the polarization. Each wing discovered the need to organize itself more tightly as a power bloc and fight the opposition more ably and consistently. This finding, coupled with the ambiguous findings concerning education on race and conflict management, raises questions about the claim that the Alinsky controversy was a successful example of "education through encounter." The educational results seem to have been highly ambiguous.

Similarly, the controversy did not have any clear-cut or uniformly positive effect on the personal relations and interaction of Bay Area Presbyterians. In our earlier interviews with presbytery leaders, we consistently heard two divergent opinions: that the conflict had produced a new degree of openness, honesty, and maturity and that it had produced a sense of bitterness, resentment, and alienation among church members. We asked a series of questions to test these opinions, and our results are interesting. In the first place, an overwhelming majority of informants felt that there had been negligible change or none at all. Secondly, among the minority (roughly 25 percent) which did suggest that change had taken place, the predominant feeling was that the change had been in the direction of rancor and evasiveness rather than candor and honesty. Specifically, the most often cited aftereffect was "distrust." Opponents were seen as bad, or at best extremely gullible men. Finally, there was a small group of informants who shared the opinion of the CORAR leaders that, as a result of the controversy, the church is now a more honest and mature institution. The overall spread of opinion certainly appears to refute any argument that the controversy was justified by a marked improvement in personal relations. It seems probable that most of the presbytery leaders' positive and negative evaluations were polemical rather than objective, i.e., they reflected approval or disapproval of the proposal rather than accurate observations concerning the results. Still, with the sole exception of the Christ Church congregation, the preponderant feeling was that the debate was either unproductive or counterproductive for relationships.

At least some quantifiable evidence exists to support a finding of alienation. The clearest instance, of course, is the loss of seventy members by Fargo. Since these members were relatively wealthy, the budget suffered a catastrophic loss. Although Westminster lost fewer (perhaps ten or twelve) members during the Alinsky battle, it also experienced a grave decline in pledges. The congregation was running $50,000 behind its "bare bones" budget for the first half of 1967, and at least $30,000 of the loss was held to be related to the Alinsky dispute. In the other four congregations, no measurable decrease in membership or pledges could be detected. Nevertheless, the pastors at both Pleasant Ridge and Evangelical were certain that their congregations' giving to the Fifty Million Fund had been cut to a fraction of what it might have been.

Having reached rather "disappointing" conclusions concerning the impact of the Alinsky controversy on such interchurch matters as education and relationships, we now turn to the question of the results for the larger community. Our hypothesis was that the failure to invite Alinsky was compensated by certain spin-off programs, which benefited the ghetto communities. Doubtless the controversy gave rise to a number of such programs. The following list is a summary of the spin-off effects:

1. At Pleasant Ridge—no specific programs; alleged general increase in mission activity, particularly in the Lexington ghetto; counterbalanced by increased alienation.
2. At Evangelical—Christians for Equality, a church-centered community organization (now defunct); police-clergy conference (now defunct); aid to Opportunities Industrial Center; generally increased involvement in racial arena.
3. At Westminster—Job Corps, an impressive vocational rehabilitation program; involvement in Urban Planning Department; increase of church Task Forces related to race and poverty programs.
4. At Fargo—membership in Fargo Community Organization, whose goals are open housing and integration; marked overall increase in mission activities.
5. At Christ Church—TOO, a fund-raising organization to sponsor training of a community organizer; coffeehouse; increased awareness of social needs.
6. At Park Street—increased support for Park Area Community Organization (PACO).

We were unable to do follow-up research on these spin-off programs. The most vital group is probably PACO. Fargo Community Organization may become significant. Job Corps and OIC have had some success but are felt to be inadequate. The others have tended to fall by the wayside. On the whole, the various spin-off programs have not had a dramatic impact on the race problems in the Bay Area. Although they may have had certain limited successes and salutary effects of involving Presbyterians in the racial arena, they have not accomplished much for the Negro communities.

A second question concerns the effect of the presbytery actions on attitudes and opinions within the ghettos. At the time of the original proposal, it was hoped that Negroes would be encouraged to look upon the Presbyterian Church and perhaps the entire Christian church as potential allies rather than enemies. For a number of reasons this hope was not fulfilled. The first and simplest reason is that few Negroes knew anything about the decisions. The second reason is that many who did follow the events felt that the June 7 decision was a sellout, another example of the "white establishment's big talk and no action." The final reason involves a historical irony. In early 1966, before Black Power had become clearly visible, Alinsky had the most radical program going. Subsequently, however, Carmichael–Rapp Brown–Karenza & Co. have stolen the show from Alinsky and, in fact, made it difficult for him to organize ghettos. Thus, reading these later developments back into 1966, some Negroes have come to feel that the entire effort was an attempt to manipulate the ghettos and to impose a "Honkey" on them. These remarks do not imply that Negroes were totally unimpressed by the Presbyterian effort. The simple fact is that little decisive change resulted in relations between the church and the ghettos.

Finally, we come to the question of how to explain the differences in congregational response. Obviously, with only six examples to draw upon, we are not able to suggest any hard and fast causal relationships between different background factors and response patterns. Nevertheless, some generalizations are possible. In general there is a correlation between socioeconomic standing and response.

TABLE 6. RANKING: WEALTH AND STATUS COMPARED
WITH RESPONSE

Wealth & Status	Opposition to Alinsky
1. Pleasant Ridge	1. Pleasant Ridge
2. Evangelical	2. Evangelical
3. Christ Church	3. Westminster
4. Fargo	4. Fargo
5. Westminster	5. Christ Church
6. Park Street	6. Park Street

Responses of the more extreme congregations are predictable on socioeconomic grounds. Furthermore, the apparently surprising response of Christ Church may be partly explained by a situational variable of basically socioeconomic nature, namely, the presence of many highly educated scientists and technicians. Nevertheless, it appears that socioeconomic factors do not adequately explain the responses of the three "middle class" congregations.

Similarly, the factor of "theological orientation" is only partially helpful. The "churchly-worldly" theology scale, like the socioeconomic rating, predicts three of the responses, but fails on the other three.

	Churchly	Worldly	Both
1. Pleasant Ridge	X		
2. Evangelical			X
3. Westminster			X
4. Fargo			X
5. Christ Church		X	
6. Park Street		X	

In other words, this scale fails to predict the strongly anti-Alinsky response of Evangelical or to explain the difference both in attitude and intensity between Westminster and Fargo. The "concept of mission" scale is somewhat more helpful.

	Individual	Mainly Individual	Both	Mainly Corporate	Corporate
1. Pleasant Ridge	X				
2. Evangelical		X			
3. Westminster		X			
4. Fargo			X		
5. Christ Church			X		
6. Park Street				X	

In particular it helps to explain why Evangelical, despite its emphasis upon mission, opposed Alinsky so strongly. This scale, however, fails to account for the clear divergence between Evangelical and Westminster and between Christ Church and Fargo.

A third set of variables which might explain the difference was "prior exposure to conflict." Like socioeconomic and theological factors, the bare amount of past conflict did not explain the response distribution.

	Negligible	Moderate	Substantial	Extensive
1. Pleasant Ridge	X			
2. Evangelical			X	
3. Westminster			X	
4. Fargo	X			
5. Christ Church		X		
6. Park Street				X

Specifically, why did Evangelical, despite its prior experience with conflict, have a harder time than Westminster? Even more, why did Christ Church, with only moderate exposure, have an easier time than Westminster and Fargo? Our findings indicate that the simple act of "throwing them in the water" will not ensure rapid improvement in swimming. Evidently there is more to it than mere *quantity* of exposure to conflict. This "something more" has to do with the *quality* of the congregations' experiences with conflict and brings us to the variables that are most helpful in explaining the congregational responses.

In appraising the responses of the congregations, we have discussed three different but interrelated matters: ability to avoid sheer, uncontrollable explosion, ability to keep the discussion focused on real issues and, of course, attitude toward Alinsky. Congregations most opposed to Alinsky obviously have the most powerful anger toward CORAR's proposal. Yet within this limitation there are certain apparent anomolies which must be explained. First, why did Westminster, with greater than 90 percent opposition, have lower intensity and better issue-focus than Pleasant Ridge and Evangelical? Second, why did Christ Church, despite a 35 percent opposition group, have such low intensity and excellent issue-focus? Third, why did Fargo, with a sixty-forty division against the proposal, have a harder time than either Westminster, which was more opposed, or Christ Church, which was also heavily split? In short, why was the discussion "better" than expected at Westminster and Christ Church and worse at Fargo?

Answers to these questions are to be found in the last two interrelated factors: pastoral leadership and attitudes toward conflict. These two variables are particularly important. First, pastoral leadership is of utmost importance in explaining why Westminster has consistently upset our predictions. Westminster's staff responded to the unpalatable proposal not simply by asserting its opposition. On the contrary, the staff carefully explained that the proposal was, in fact, an effort by sincere Christians to respond to an urgent need. Thus, rather than mere protest, the duty of other Christians was to work out a better alternative. This response caused the emotional reaction to subside quickly and the discussion to take a creative turn. Another factor of considerable importance for Westminster was the ability of the multiple (five-man) staff to develop a division of labor which facilitated problem-focus.

How did this exercise of pastoral leadership differ from the other congregations? In Pleasant Ridge, the pastor refused both to interpret the opposition and to focus the discussions on substantive issues, such as alternatives. In fact, he refused to enter the discussion at all. At Evangelical, the pastors did seek to discuss alternatives, but they were unwilling to interpret the CORAR position as in any way justifiable, and they therefore gave license to extreme anger against the opposition. Similarly, the pastors at Fargo and Park Street participated only on one side of the debate. The pastor at Fargo is the only one who took a position in opposition to the majority of his parishioners. This might not have been disastrous, except that he refused to let the majority decide the matter. Finally, the pastor at Christ Church, like Westminster, approved of both sides of the debate as rational positions. Christ Church, furthermore, had a multiple staff which it was able to marshall effectively. The real key to Christ Church's success, however, lay in earlier leadership which the pastor had provided in the area of church conflict.

Early in his ministry Mr. Sharp, of Christ Church, recognized that structural changes in the parish would be necessary to move the church into a new era. Chiefly, he attempted to encourage lay involvement and specialization by means of a complete structural reorganization. After the change, however, Mr. Sharp became cognizant of one major weakness, namely, that there was no official channel for the airing of conflict. Since conflict was in the wind, the church leaders decided to devote the entire annual retreat of that year (1966) to the question of how to handle the conflict. Thus, although no formal structure emerged, the congregation had begun to consider the problem. When the conflict broke, Mr. Sharp responded by inviting all members of the congregation to express their feelings in a series of open session meetings. In short, Mr. Sharp created an *ad hoc* structure for airing the conflicting viewpoints.

Although these minimal efforts at conflict management cannot be viewed as revolutionary, their effect seems to have been quite marked. Despite a dangerous 65–35 split in the congregation, there was no explosion and no dysfunctional conflict. Thus, we would argue that Christ Church is the most forceful example of the importance of both pastoral leadership and structural readiness in the creative handling of conflict.

Our data provide two more illustrations of the importance of appropriate attitudes and structures for dealing with conflict. The first is the "Concerns of the Church" period in Park Street's Sunday services. During these sessions the entire membership is encouraged to express honest feelings about the various church activities. In addition the members have learned to accept their "opponents" on different issues in a spirit of friendliness. Although this machinery was not severely tested by the Alinsky proposal, its performance in recent years has been impressive. Park Street has learned to incorporate conflict as part of its normal ongoing life.

The second and even more striking example ironically concerns Fargo. There, a group known as Parish Communicant Education (PCE) went far toward proving the value of institutional structures for the expression of conflict. The purpose of PCE was educational, but in the course of its discussions the members became involved in heated debates. The effect, as one participant put it, was that "we never did resolve the disagreement, but we did come to accept each other. From then on our group felt more like a family. We felt as though we could say anything." When the storm broke over Alinsky and despite the pullout of seventy members, *not one* of the conservative (anti-Alinsky) participants in PCE left the church. By facing the fact of conflict, they had learned that they could live with people who disagreed with them.

Summary: Purge, Schism, or Pluralism

The fundamental finding of our study is that the already polarized Presbyterian Church of the Bay Area became nearly "schizophrenic" under the duress of the battle over Saul Alinsky in 1966. The events of that year revealed that the church has two separate and nearly unrelated personalities, and that the confrontation of the two can bring the activities of the entire group to a standstill. In the aftermath of the Alinsky controversy, the two factions faced each other with open and unabashed hostility. Each considered the other to be basically unchristian. The lines of communication were completely broken down. Each faction seemed more determined than ever to fight and *defeat* its enemies within the church.

In such a situation, what can be done? The first option is to purge the *liberal* staff bodies and clergy who cause trouble by pushing for radical action. Basically this is the hope and intention of many of the more conservative individuals interviewed. They feel that the entire direction of the new breed of activists has been wrong. They hope, through the conservative-oriented Presbyterian Lay Committee, pulpit committees, and increased vigilance, to reverse the trend and return the church to the spiritual arena where it belongs.

A second option is to get rid of the *conservative* "obstructionists." Two basic possibilities are involved: schism or gradual "burning off." The controversy over Alinsky was definitely intense enough to produce warnings of incipient schism. At Fargo, of course, a schism actually occurred. In addition, there was talk at Pleasant Ridge, Evangelical, Westminster, and an indefinite number of other churches concerning possible corporate withdrawal from presbytery or massive individual withdrawals. A method preferred by some liberals for getting rid of the conservatives is referred to as "burning off." The idea is that a gradual acceleration of social action will cause a few conservatives at a time to pull out and will leave a moderate-to-liberal remnant capable of effective social action. This is what has happened over the years at Park Street.

A third option is to find a way for Presbyterians to live together creatively in spite of their substantial differences. In view of the utter failure to work together during the Alinsky furor, it seems obvious that *major* attitudinal and structural changes would be required in order to achieve this third possibility.

This book takes the position that the third option, despite its difficulty, is the one that should be adopted. This argument is based on the following assumptions. First and most significantly, we feel that each of the two factions is stressing an indispensable aspect of the Christian religion. Ministry to the church and the world, comfort and challenge, maintenance and mission, worship and action—in each case, *both* of these pairs are unavoidable parts of a whole and healthy Christian church. Either one without the other is less than fully Christian. One without the other leads to a truncated church. Second, we feel that the interaction between the two aspects of Christianity has been and can continue to be creative rather than destructive. It seems that liberals need conservatives to challenge them to be authentic in their liberalism and vice versa. Third and related to the above two points, we feel that either faction by itself would be useless. The activists alone might be willing to act, but they would lack power or money base for effective action. The conservatives alone would drift into self-indulgent isolation and protection of self-interest.

In short, the tension that church members feel today is an indication of the nature of Christianity, not a sign of disease. The challenge is to appropriate the tension so that it will spur rather than destroy the institution. We feel that today's crisis is the result of the flabby one-sidedness of Christianity in the fifties and the exaggerated ardor of the new breed of Worldly Christians in the sixties. It represents the growing pains in the church's coming back into its own. The final part of this book is an attempt to provide some constructive guidelines toward living together in a frankly pluralistic church.

9

A New Look at Church Conflict

The increasing number of conflict situations confronting religious groups has given rise to suggestions that the church should reevaluate its attitude toward conflict and its tools for coping with controversial issues. Such reappraisal is essential as churches have traditionally feared and fled from conflict in quest of harmony and reconciliation.

Since the days ahead will likely see more intensified conflict, it stands to reason that the church must develop new attitudes and structures to cope with the situation it will surely have to face. If our analysis is correct, the church has become so polarized that it may be called schizophrenic. During the Alinsky controversy of 1966, the church was severely split, and the division has not subsequently been healed. Furthermore, our interpretation has shown that whether local congregations could handle controversy constructively or not was related to their experiences with and attitudes toward conflict.

This chapter spells out a revised attitude toward conflict situations. We shall argue, first of all, that conflict is an unavoidable *fact* of church life, one that can be ignored only at grave peril. Secondly, we shall attempt to demonstrate that the fact of conflict can be an *opportunity* rather than simply a reason for dismay. Finally, we shall contend that one of the chief causes of the church's schizophrenia has been its failure to develop adequate tools for *conflict management,* and that the benefits which may flow from conflict will be lost unless the church increases its expertise in this area.

CONFLICT: A FACT

After the "spiral of controversy" during the past few years in the life of Bay Area Presbyterians, it seems like a classic understatement to mention that conflict is a "fact" of church life. Even before the Alinsky controversy exploded, many churchmen had received a large taste of conflict.

Park Street had already come to think of conflict as "doing what comes naturally." Westminister had been exposed to an "upward spiral of controversy." Evangelical had had at least three highly charged debates. Christ Church, despite only two serious controversies, had begun to set up actual structures for handling conflict. Even Pleasant Ridge and Fargo had managed to avoid outbursts only by precariously skirting the growing feelings of animosity among their members.

If any doubt remained about the reality of conflict, it was put to rest in the spring of 1966. During the days that followed the proposal to finance Alinsky, the only two of our six churches that escaped intense controversy were Park Street and Christ Church, the two that favored the decision and that had already accepted conflict as an inescapable dimension of parish life. The latent hostility of the Pleasant Ridge and Fargo members was brought suddenly to the surface, and these congregations were face to face with their first major conflicts. The uneasy peace at Westminster and Evangelical was again disrupted. And the presbytery itself was precipitated into the most explosive episode of its entire history.

Yet how can we be certain that these events were not merely passing phases in the life of the church? Even after the Alinsky debate had run its course, nearly 15 percent of our informants were of the opinion that conflict is a "sign that something is wrong" with the church. Would it not be possible for the church to settle down again, resolve its differences, and restore calm to its troubled waters? The answer, we submit, is that hopes such as these are certain to be disappointed. Conflict is a reality of life that the church cannot and must not try to escape. This contention is not merely an empirical observation; rather, it is a fundamental theoretical conclusion supported by theologians, psychiatrists, and sociologists alike.

Theologically, the fact of conflict is an extremely simple inference from the doctrine of original sin. This much-maligned doctrine may be taken at the very least to mean that man is almost unavoidably self-centered. Self-interest appears to be the most dominant human motivation; and when the interests of different individuals clash, conflict ensues. Reinhold Niebuhr has given one of the most cogent descriptions of man's conflict-producing nature. In *Moral Man and Immoral Society,* he rebutted the bland optimism of the Social Gospel by demonstrating that humans, particularly in their group life, are inevitably caught up in the clash of self-interest. Paul Tillich, in *Love, Power, and Justice,* has echoed this finding and attempted to reveal its metaphysical rootage. In his opinion, love must be complemented by power that seeks to destroy that which is against love. Even the exponents of "reconciliation" recognize that there must be conflict before reconciliation can be had.

Among the psychiatrists, Freud has most emphatically supported the contention of the theologians that conflict is unavoidable. On the basis of his studies, he was driven to the conclusion that conflict is basic to the human organism. More significantly, however, conflict exists between the desires of the individual and the demands of society. As civilization becomes more complicated, this tension becomes progressively more pronounced. Finally, Freud was forced to posit an innate drive toward destructiveness that places man in constant opposition to others and to himself.

Even sociologists, with their partiality for conflict-free models of human society, have had to face the fact of conflict.

Georg Simmel, one of the pioneers of German sociology, has argued that the "primary human need" for hostility and the inescapable clash of objective interests make tension and conflict necessary features of human group life. Although many sociologists have ignored Simmel's findings, Ralf Dahrendorf has recently argued for the adoption of a "conflict-model" of society. As he sees it, social life per se implies conflict, and we should assume that if there is *no* conflict, something is wrong. Indeed, the only place where there is an absence of conflict is the graveyard.

Simmel's analysis in particular provides an extremely interesting insight into conflict within the church. We have noted that Simmel viewed conflict as the clash of individuals seeking commodities that they value, and when there are not enough of these commodities to go around, then the individuals will come into conflict with each other. One of the reasons that the church has been able to avoid conflict is that its principal commodity is the grace of God, which by definition is sufficient for everyone. The bestowal of grace on one person does not diminish the supply available to others. As the church moves into the political and social arena, however, it begins to deal in scarce commodities, and it comes face to face with conflict.

Our own analysis of the "two faces of organized religion" helps to shed light on these theoretical conclusions concerning conflict. We have argued that the church rests on a fundamental dualism or goal ambivalence which may be depicted as follows:

	Churchly	*Worldly*
1. Relation to secular society	Support	Criticize
2. Relation to members	Comfort	Challenge

Furthermore, we have argued that the contemporary church is divided into "churchly" and "worldly" factions which, in addition to the fundamental dualism, have the following divergent attitudes:

3. Attitude toward institutional church	Maintenance	Risk
4. Main purpose of church	Worship, prayer, Bible study	Mission
5. Concept of mission	Individual to individual	Exercise of corporate power
6. Style	Harmony	Conflict

A look at this list of six characteristics reveals that each pair is in some degree of tension. Our argument, however, has been that each of the two poles represents a legitimate and important function of the church. Thus, to the degree that conflict is absent in the life of the church, the inference can be drawn that the church is ignoring at least one of its duties. Conflict should be seen as a sign that the church is doing what it should be doing. Twenty-five percent of our informants acknowledged this fact by calling conflict at worst a "necessary evil" in the life of the church.

CONFLICT: AN OPPORTUNITY

We need not stop with the conclusion that conflict is an unavoidable fact of church life. Rather, we are prepared to argue that conflict may be positively beneficial both for the church as an institution and for individual Christians. As Alfred North Whitehead put it, "The clash of doctrine is not a disaster, it is an opportunity." Certainly that is not a new idea. On the contrary, 60 percent of our informants felt that conflict within the church is a "positive sign." Nevertheless, the commonsense opinion is still widely held that conflict is basically a disruptive and divisive force, a force that should be avoided whenever possible. We wish to explain why the commonsense notion is wrong and how conflict works to the benefit of the groups and individuals involved.

The first important question is how conflict benefits group life. This process has been best described by the two "sociologists of conflict," Georg Simmel and Lewis Coser. Simmel was perhaps the first to state in unequivocal terms that conflict serves as a cement which holds groups together. In his classic work *Conflict*, he attempted to demonstrate the mechanisms that allow conflict to bind groups together rather than to tear them apart.* Coser, in *The Functions of Conflict*, has succinctly restated this proposition as follows:

> Groups require disharmony as well as harmony, dissociation as well as association; and conflicts within them are by no means altogether disruptive factors. . . . The belief that one process tears down what the other builds up, so that what finally remains is the result of subtracting the one from the other, is based on a misconception. . . . Far from being necessarily dysfunctional, a certain degree of conflict is an essential element in group formation and the persistence of group life.

For purposes of this discussion, we shall present five basic propositions derived from Simmel and Coser that illustrate how conflict serves group life:

1. Conflict allows members to express hostility that otherwise might lead to withdrawal or to accumulation and explosion.
2. Conflict allows the group to get a clear picture of its own needs and to adjust itself accordingly.
3. Conflict creates new groups.
4. Conflict with other groups (outgroups) helps to provide

---

* For sociological literature on conflict, see Lewis Coser, *The Functions of Social Conflict* (The Free Press of Glencoe, Inc., 1956); James S. Coleman, *Community Conflict* (The Free Press of Glencoe, Inc., 1957); Georg Simmel, *Conflict* (The Free Press of Glencoe, Inc., 1955); Ralf Dahrendorf, "Out of Utopia: Towards a Reorientation of Sociological Analysis," *American Journal of Sociology*, 64 (1958), pp. 115–127; and Peter Rossi, "Community Decision Making," *Administrative Science Quarterly*, March, 1957.

a sense of group (ingroup) identity and to increase internal cohesion.

5. Conflict binds antagonists together.

The first proposition is that conflict "clears the air." Group life, as we all know, necessarily gives rise to tensions, antagonisms, and hostilities. If these negative feelings are not expressed, they work underground in a divisive and destructive way. The gossip and the backbiting that go on within many churches under a facade of fellowship and goodwill are obvious to all who are honest enough to admit it. If hostility is allowed to build up over too long a period, it may lead members to withdraw from the group or produce a single powerful explosion in which all the accumulated feeling bursts forth uncontrollably. The clearest case in point is marriage. The importance of the marriage relationship and the consequent fear of harming or losing it produce a strong tendency to conceal hostility. When the anger does come to the surface, the viciousness of the marital fight may be quite astonishing. If, on the other hand, irritation is expressed when it occurs, the underground accumulation does not take place. For this reason, many institutions create "safety valves" which allow members to vent their hostility against someone outside the group. Such scapegoating, of course, finds its classic expression in anti-Semitism. The safety valve acts as a "lightning rod" that releases immediate tensions, but it does not resolve the underlying problem that gave rise to the hostility. Thus, Simmel and Coser are led to suggest that groups should encourage the immediate and direct expression of antagonism and provide channels for such expression. By removing the tension as it occurs, the group can preserve integration and cohesion.

The Alinsky controversy was undoubtedly a negative illustration of the operation of the principle. Hostility had been brewing for years on the question of church involvement in the social and political arena, but expression of feelings was not encouraged, and no channels existed for genuine confrontation. This was particularly true for the members of the Pleasant Ridge and Fargo congregations. It was also the case at Westminster and Evangelical and for the presbytery at large. Finally, when an issue came that could not be sidestepped, the pent-up anger burst forth and became totally uncontrollable.

The second proposition is that conflict allows a group to gain a clear picture of its present needs and desires and to adjust itself so that it can meet them better. The experience of Dr. Hope at Westminster during the Proposition 14 debate is a perfect illustration of this principle. The expression of anger by the congregation gave Dr. Hope an accurate reading of the attitudes of his parishioners and helped him to adjust his ministry to their situation. Frequently, as the composition of a group changes, the old structures and programs become ill-fitted to the new situation and cease to promote the ongoing group life. In such a situation, conflict may be helpful to indicate the relative strength of the different interests and the changes that are needed.

Conflict not only aids the adjustment of existing groups, however. As the third proposition points out, it may actually give rise to new groups. In the Alinsky controversy, for example, the Ad Hoc Appeals Committee was born. This group provided significant contacts between formerly unacquainted members of eighteen different congregations, and it exists, although in attenuated form, to this day.

The fourth proposition presented by Simmel and Coser is that conflict increases the internal group cohesion and sense of identity if the conflict is with an external "enemy" rather than an internal adversary. The classic illustration of this principle is Stalin's use of the "capitalist encirclement" propaganda in unifying the youthful U.S.S.R. The tendency of outgroup conflict to unify the ingroup is so great that groups will frequently seek out an enemy to do battle with. The operation of this "group-binding" tendency was clearly present in the Alinsky controversy. The forces of Churchly Christianity achieved a much higher degree of internal cohesion, and some individuals even attempted to institutionalize their position in the Presbyterian Lay Committee. Similarly, the Worldly Christians at Park Street got a clear sense of their solidarity with individuals in other churches and of the importance of unified action in pursuing their goals. In this case, however, since the "enemies" were members of the same institution, the overall effect was polarization.

The fifth proposition is an interesting one, namely, that conflict can even bind together the antagonists. To carry on conflict there must be some sort of relationship even if it is antagonistic. Frequently, the act of opposing a person is the first encounter with him. Thus, the conflict provides a chance to test the opponent and get to know him. The encounter may reveal some of the opponent's good points and lay the basis for a future cooperative relationship. In many cases, according to Simmel and Coser, opponents will emerge from a conflict with the feeling that it has become easier rather than more difficult to relate to each other and work with each other. We attempted to test for this result, but although we found that the Alinsky controversy did introduce antagonists to each other, most of our informants felt that it had become harder to work with their opponents. Thus, the divisive aspects seem to have outweighed the integrative ones in this case.

In the preceding paragraphs, we have attempted to explain some of the ways in which conflict can be beneficial to group life. The next question that we propose to discuss is how conflict can be helpful to the individual. Most Christians would agree that their religion places great emphasis on love. The image of a "good Christian" is that of a loving person; consequently, expressions of anger and hatred seem from a superficial viewpoint to be unchristian. In fact, many Christians suffer from guilt even when they become aware of *feelings* of anger and hatred. Yet psychiatry has told us that love and hatred are closely bound together, that the loving relationship is an ambivalent one that includes elements of hatred as well. Many churchmen, in their desire to be loving, have denied their own negative feelings and have substituted a sort of undifferentiated kindness for genuine love. By suppressing their negative feelings, they have gotten out of touch with their positive feelings as well.

A recent trend in some church circles that attempts to counter this situation is the use of the encounter group or T-group. The encounter group brings its members together once a week or more for gatherings in which the focus is on honest and open expression of whatever feelings the individuals may have. Needless to say, it is possible for the encounter group to give rise to extremely intense personal conflicts as hostilities are brought to the surface. The experience can be astonishing for at least two reasons: first, the members are often shocked to discover vast amounts of intense anger of which they had little awareness, and, second, the members frequently find that after purging themselves of this hostility they are able to love and support each other in ways much more profound than before. In short, by getting in touch with their own resentments and expressing them, the members are also able to get in touch with dimensions of love that make their former "good nature and loving-kindness" seem superficial indeed. Furthermore, in terms of their relationships with others, they find that powerful anger can coexist with love.

The Episcopal Church in the Bay Area has recently begun to use the device of encounter groups to open up communication among its members and to encourage the expression of animosities that might otherwise undermine its group life. They have found that the honest expression of feeling can have beneficial results for both the churchly and the worldly aspects of religion. In terms of community worship, they are applying the principle voiced by Christ that you should not worship together until you have come to terms with your anger toward your brothers. The open expression of conflict and the *subsequent* reconciliation can give rise to a sense of community which can make worship a truly exalting experience. In terms of mission, the Episcopal Church is finding similarly beneficial results. Members are coming to terms with the fact that they can work together in complementary ways despite major differences of opinion. The fact, as we have argued, is that many disagreements are specious. They result from seeing complementary jobs as mutually exclusive. What individuals can discover is that different emphases and styles of operation do not necessarily imply different ultimate goals.

In short, what we have attempted to demonstrate is that conflict can be beneficial for individuals as well as for groups, and that it can enhance both the churchly and the worldly aspects of Christianity. If, as we have argued, conflict is such a beneficial process, then why are our conclusions so negative with respect to the Alinsky conflict? Certainly "gap," "polarization," "alienation," and even "schizophrenia" are not benefits. This question brings us to the heart of our discussion of conflict. Conflict, as we shall see, is only beneficial if it is "managed" properly.

CONFLICT MANAGEMENT: A NECESSITY

A fundamental assumption underlying our analysis is that the dynamics of conflict are autonomous. It is important that we understand what this assumption means. Conflict by *its very nature* sets into operation a predictable series of developments that take place wholly apart from any human plan or intention. They represent the natural life cycle of a conflict. Furthermore, these autonomous tendencies are potentially dangerous: they carry the conflict toward increasing intensity and polarization. In short, when we say that the dynamics of conflict are autonomous, we mean that conflict itself has a kind of inner imperative to unfold in predictable (and often precarious) ways.

Although Coser has provided some helpful analysis on this point, the most thorough treatment is given by James Coleman in his monograph entitled *Community Conflict*. Coleman

studied a large number of community conflict situations
and came to the conclusion that, apart from any intention
of the parties, conflict has a strong tendency to unfold as
follows:

1. An issue is presented.
2. The issue disrupts the equilibrium of community relations.
3. Previously suppressed issues come to the surface.
4. More and more of the opponents' beliefs enter the disagreement.
5. The opponents appear totally bad.
6. Charges are made against the opponents as persons.
7. The dispute becomes independent of the original disagreement.

During this process, a number of critical developments tend
to take place. First, the definition of the issues changes from
specific to general. Then new issues come into the debate, issues that may be closely related or nearly unrelated to the
original issue. Gradually antagonism replaces disagreement.
Since it is more comfortable psychologically to see the opponent as totally bad, the antagonism increases to a point of total
personal animosity. At the same time, changes take place in
the social organization of the parties. Relationships among opponents whither away, and the community becomes polarized.
Ad hoc combat groups are formed to replace the more com-
promising permanent institutions. Radical leaders emerge and
begin a process of propaganda and demagoguery. The normal
channels of communication break down, and the combatants
increasingly receive information through unreliable word-of-
mouth communication. In short, the conflict situation moves
toward maximum intensity and polarization. Pulling no
punches, Coleman emphasizes that the spiral is very likely to
occur because communities are usually not able to develop
optimal procedures for handling conflict. In the absence of
such procedures, dangerous elements are able to drive out

more stable ones, and the conflict becomes a mutual attempt to ruin the opponents.

To restate what we have said before: these developments are autonomous, they tend to occur spontaneously in every major community conflict. At this point, however, we shall introduce our second fundamental assumption: the cycle of intensification and polarization is *not inevitable*. If these patterns can be broken, then the conflict can be channeled into more constructive paths. The obvious fact, however, is that the dangerous cycles can only be broken by conscious decision and effort. In other words, conflict will tend to go out of control unless the group *plans* how to manage it. The positive functions of conflict discussed above may be forfeited unless there is "conflict management" in the form either of prior controls or determined interventions in the actual conflict. Since we have argued that conflict is unavoidable for the church, it becomes important to determine whether the church has adequate attitudes toward and tools for conflict management. We shall do so by considering the course of the Alinsky controversy in terms of Coleman's description. Coleman's analysis was based on conflicts in "communities" such as towns and cities. Thus it is not obvious that his findings would apply to subcommunities such as the church. As we shall see, however, the parallels in the Alinsky controversy were very marked.

The controversy began when CORAR presented the initial issue whether the presbytery should provide $200,000 to support two action projects by Saul Alinsky and the Industrial Areas Foundation. Community relations were immediately and severely disrupted. Two major suppressed issues that had been brewing for years were surfaced, namely, the anger of the conservatives over the question of church involvement in social and political issues and their frustration over the way liberals were "running the presbytery and walking all over" their conservative brethren. Before long the opponents were seeing each other as totally bad. Alinsky, CORAR, the Ad Hoc group, and leaders on both sides became dirty words among various circles. Personal charges were made. Rumors flew. And soon the dispute had become diverted from the initial issue.

At the same time, the issues shifted from specific (Alinsky, race relations) to general (nature of the church). New issues came to the fore including notably CORAR's tactics. Antagonism replaced disagreement and severe polarization set in. The conciliatory voice of the General Council was shoved into the background, and the two combat groups (CORAR and the Ad Hoc group) with their committed leaders faced each other in open hostility. In short, the conflict followed precisely the course predicted by Coleman.

If, as we have argued, these developments were not inevitable and might have been avoided through conflict management, then the question arises whether any attempt was made to prepare for or intervene in the conflict. In the first place, CORAR seems to have had little sensitivity to the importance of conflict management. It was believed that the simple fact of exposure to conflict would be a good experience for the church. As we have seen, however, this notion is probably mistaken: *how* conflict is handled appears to be a much more significant factor than simply *how much* conflict there has been. Thus, despite early warnings, CORAR went ahead with its emergency plans and did not prepare itself adequately for the subsequent controversy. Other than a minimum attempt to distribute information and hold meetings, few plans were laid. Another mistake was the failure to consult with the mass of laity. This allowed the mass media to break the news, an event that, as Coleman predicted, had explosive consequences.

In the aftermath of April 12, CORAR tried two measures. First, they presented a "clarifying statement" at a subsequent meeting. This proved wholly inadequate. Second, they set up the "area meeting" program. This did serve to keep at least some channels of communication open. The major attempt at conflict management, of course, was the calling of the bipartisan committee and the request for reconsideration. This was simply too little, too late. The Coleman cycle had run its course, and the presbytery was hopelessly polarized. The result, as we have seen, was the "non-decision" on June 7. In order to quell the conflict presbytery *de facto* tabled the issue.

Meanwhile, conflict management within the six congregations was scarcely better. Despite the fact that the controversy was waxing hot in at least four of the six, no new procedures for coping with the situation were tried. In all four cases, complete reliance was placed on procedures that had survived from earlier days. The absence was particularly pronounced in Pleasant Ridge and Fargo. The former simply refused to discuss the issue at all, while the latter, trying to cope with a long-standing but previously unacknowledged split, literally fell to pieces.

Our conclusion is that the presbytery and the local congregations did poorly in their exercise of conflict management and that this may explain why the conflict had such divisive effects. In view of the unavoidability of conflict, this poses a serious problem for the church. Perhaps we can shed light both on the events of 1966 and the way to proceed from here if we discuss some of the established "techniques" of conflict management and point out their presence or absence in the Alinsky debate. We shall consider three major techniques: institutionalization, multiple memberships, and leadership responses.

Probably the most significant method of conflict management is "institutionalization" or the provision of a permanent forum in which complaints and controversies can be aired as they arise. As Coser puts it, "Institutionalized channels for carrying out such conflicts would seem to constitute an important 'balancing mechanism' in a society." Coleman similarly stresses the importance of "procedures of dissent." The advantages of such forums for conflict are evident. First, they allow expression rather than accumulation of antagonism. Second, they allow the group to gain experience in facing conflict over minor matters, experience which becomes vitally important in handling serious conflicts. Third, they inculcate the readiness to intervene appropriately in conflict situations and to redirect the dynamics of the situation in constructive ways.

In the Alinsky debate, such institutions were almost entirely absent. At the presbytery level, there was no adequate forum for working out the conflict. The only official forum for confrontation was the presbytery meetings. These meetings have traditionally been concerned with administrative matters and have provided limited practice in dealing with conflict. In the absence of a permanent institution for managing the conflict, it was necessary to fall back on the temporary bipartisan committee, and even that expedient was only invoked after more than two weeks of unrestrained conflict. In the congregations, as we have seen, the situation was equally bad. Four of the congregations had literally no forum for facing conflict. Pleasant Ridge and Evangelical had no tools at all, and they escaped disaster only because of the unanimity of their members. Westminster, despite its substantial exposure to conflict situations, had failed to develop any actual forum for airing differences. Finally, it was Fargo that found itself most poorly prepared and that suffered most heavily. The absence of institutional means for handling conflict becomes even more clear when we recall that despite the intensity of the Alinsky controversy, no new methods were tried in any of these four churches or in the presbytery. In the preceding chapter, we have discussed the salutary effect of Christ Church's retreat and open session meetings, Fargo's "Parish Communicant Education," and Park Street's "Concerns" period during the worship service. These examples forcefully illustrate the importance of "institutionalizing" conflict.

The second major technique of conflict management is to develop an interdependence among antagonists through crosscutting group memberships. This method, suggested both by Coleman and Coser, serves to prevent a polarization of the group along one main line of cleavage. If opponents are represented on the various subcommittees, then continuous expression of minor grievances is ensured, and it becomes more difficult for a pure group versus group split to occur. This method is also called co-optation, wherein key individuals, frequently opponents, are invited to share in decision-making. As far as we know, this technique was not consciously adopted in any of our churches or in the presbytery. Thus, for example, CORAR was made up almost entirely of action-oriented clergymen and laymen, and the opponents found it nearly impossible to voice their dissent within this structure. Similarly, the Ad Hoc Appeals Committee had only strongly anti-Alinsky members.

The most flagrant example of a failure to implement cross-cutting memberships was at Fargo. There the entire congregation was divided into groups that held fundamentally divergent attitudes and pursued wholly different programs. Furthermore, these groups were almost totally out of touch with each other. The structural split that paralleled the attitudinal split was so complete that the two wings even had separate worship services. Thus, when the conflict began, there was an already existing polarization that simply surfaced and hardened. Whatever relations might have existed between the two groups withered, and the congregation split in two. Presumably, if our analysis is correct, Fargo might have taken steps to bring the two wings into communication and confrontation, and—as the PCE experience suggests—the rupture might have been ameliorated.

The third technique of conflict management concerns leadership responses. Coser argues that conflicts can be either "realistic" or "nonrealistic." A realistic conflict is one which concerns objective issues, whereas a nonrealistic conflict is predominantly a vehicle for the expression of personal animosity. Thus, the function of the leader or mediator, according to Coser, is to divest the conflict of its nonrealistic aspects and get it back to the objective issue. This opinion, which squares with Coleman's analysis of the dynamics of controversy, has also been stressed by Dan Dodson and his coauthors. They feel that the critical component of conflict management is how the leaders react. Either avoidance or knocking heads will be dangerous, and the leaders must pursue a more delicate approach. The techniques that Dodson suggests include the following: articulate the objective differences of opinion, enable both sides to be heard, promote honest discussion, set ground rules, make sure that all the facts are presented, help the opponents to arrive at a decision, and evaluate the entire process after the fact. Coleman too has stressed the importance of immediate and forceful responses by the group leaders.

As stated in the preceding chapter, the presence or absence of the third technique helps us to understand the response of the various congregations, particularly the positive experiences of Christ Church and Westminster. The most notable violation of these principles occured at Pleasant Ridge, where the interim pastor made a firm decision to avoid all discussion of the issue. This allowed the congregation to focus almost entirely on nonrealistic matters such as anger at CORAR and Alinsky's personality. With no guidance from their pastor, the members were not brought into communication with their opponents and were unable to work out any differences. The conflict merely solidified their antagonism to the presbytery leaders and their determination to prevent any repeat in the future. The experience at Fargo was not much better, but at least the pastor attempted to assume some leadership in the discussion.

Although the Alinsky controversy was marked mostly by failure in conflict management, the positive instances leave some room for optimism concerning the church's ability to manage conflict creatively in the future. If our analysis is correct, then the factors that most adequately explain the different responses are those which are *in the control* of rational decisions. Thus it seems likely that with more expertise in conflict management the church will be able to handle the conflicts that seem to be an unavoidable part of its future.

10

Blueprint for a Multi-Church

Clark Kerr, former president of the University of California, has argued that the term "uni-versity" is a misnomer when applied to today's gigantic educational complexes. He suggests "multi-versity" would be more accurate. A multi-versity, according to Kerr, can be defined as a number of independent educational enterprises tied together by a common parking problem.

Similarly, our analysis of responses to the Alinsky controversy leads to the inescapable conclusion that the church is anything but the "one body of Christ." On the contrary, the church has become thoroughly pluralistic. It is composed of several groups with admittedly diverse notions concerning the nature and task of religion. In this sense, we suggest that the Presbyterian Church has become a "multi-church." It is, one might facetiously say, a collection of persons held together by a common preference for bad choir music. Life in a multi-church poses many difficult problems. Since we have argued that pluralism is preferable to purge or schism, it is necessary to suggest some guidelines for dealing with those problems. While the preceding chapter suggested a "revised attitude toward church conflict," the present chapter attempts to spell out some concrete suggestions pertaining to attitudinal changes and structural reforms.

The first prerequisite for a multi-church is a *frankly plural-*

istic theology, a theology that affirms a broad spectrum of differing programs. That is an obvious but frequently overlooked point. Thus, for example, the advocates of Worldly Christianity have been filling the air with demands for a "theology of conflict," a "theology of social change," a "theology of revolution," and so on. Meanwhile, proponents of Churchly Christianity have been insisting on a theology of inner experience, prayer, and worship. The fact of the matter, however, is that neither of these demands is apropos to the current situation. What the church needs is a "theology of both/and," a pluralistic theology broad enough to affirm the complementary nature of the different dimensions of Christianity.

Much evidence points to the necessity of a pluralistic theology. In the first place, the goals of Christianity itself are pluralistic. Thus, an authentically Christian theology must take the multiple goals into account. Secondly, unless the basic theology is broad enough to include both poles, the church will be threatened with extremely intense conflict. A well-known conclusion of conflict theory is that ideological conflicts are more radical and merciless than any other. Thirdly, both types of Christian action are appropriate and valuable in many practical situations. The racial arena provides striking confirmation of this third point. Urban crises and the cries from the ghetto have strongly confirmed the need for corporate action. The Kerner Commission Report has underlined the liberals' contention that individual evangelism is insufficient. At the same time, recent developments have indicated that the conservatives may have been closer to the truth than the liberals realized. With the emergence of Black Power, Negroes are saying to whites to get out of the ghetto and to put their own houses in order. Conservatives have been saying all along that the regeneration of white attitudes is just as critical as the sinking of vast funds into the ghettos. In short, the time has come for a clearer recognition that the polar extremes of Christian understanding offer complementary rather than mutually exclusive programs.

The attitudinal correlate of pluralistic theology is *tolerance*. Presbyterians have tended to be overly possessive about their church. They have insisted that the church undertake only those activities which they support. Thus, as one pastor argued: "The church is one body. If it is to act, it must have at least 75 percent consensus." Such a program is a charter of inaction. It is doubtful whether Bay Area Presbyterians could get 75 percent agreement on the weather. Consensus politics are obsolete in the multi-church. The time has come to create a presumption in favor of action without clear consensus along the church's multiple lines of interest. In this regard, Presbyterians could learn from the hippies' motto of allowing each person to do "his own thing." In addition, if churchmen could "take the role of the other" and make a genuine effort to see things as his "opponents" see them, then the mutual recrimination might be replaced by cooperation.

In the course of our study, we became aware of an extraordinary intolerance among various church factions. Many of our conservative informants revealed the angry vindictiveness that has become associated with the political and theological right wing. They frequently labeled their activist opponents as stupid, evil, and unchristian. Equally striking was the intolerance of the church's ultra liberals. They ridiculed and rebuked their opponents mercilessly. They too slurred the motives of the opposition and implied that the conservatives did not merit the name Christian. In the aftermath of the Alinsky debate, the conservatives were so stung by rude treatment that forgiveness, despite its prime place on the list of Christian virtues, seemed unlikely. It would appear that both sides were being parochial and somewhat childish.

The attitude of tolerance becomes particularly important with reference to the activities of denominational and regional leaders. We have argued repeatedly that the church has a dual function of criticizing and supporting the social order and of challenging and comforting its members. Furthermore, we have contended that the church is falling short if it is not performing *both* of these tasks. The consistent finding of numerous studies in the sociology of religion, however, is that the local parish tends almost unavoidably to stress its supporting and comforting roles at the expense of its duty to challenge. Thus, if the prophetic role is to be fulfilled, additional leaders are demanded. The logical contenders for the role of prophets, as the Protestant Episcopal Church and the Roman Catholic Church have discovered, are the professional staff men in the national and regional bureaucracies. Our analysis reverses the usual sociological theorem that bureaucrats will not be innovators. The new breed of church officials are likely to have greater social sensitivity. They have the time, talent, and resources to become "experts" on crucial social issues, and they have greater financial independence than the local pastor who is usually tied to the purse strings of his congregation. In short, we agree with Charles Y. Glock's suggestion that the parish is the probable center for the comfort function, and the hierarchy the logical locus of the challenge function. Consequently, we feel that CORAR, in pressing for racial action, was carrying out its legitimate function. Presbyterians should expect and encourage their staff leaders to act as prophets. We are not suggesting that the local parish should abdicate its prophetic role. The local pastor should act in both roles. We are merely recognizing the natural constraints and limits of parish action.

In our study, we found one exemplary case of the mutual tolerance being suggested. This occurred at Christ Church, where Mr. Sharp has succeeded in convincing his parishioners that "Christians" may hold quite different opinions, and that each group is entitled to try out those programs which seem fruitful. In other words, the fact that some Christians disagree with an action does not mean that the action is unchristian. More specifically, Mr. Sharp was able to persuade the congregation that CORAR has the right to try out programs even though they might not command full assent of presbytery members.

Finally, as we have said, it is urgent that churchmen change their attitudes about conflict from fear and dislike to acceptance. Life in the multi-church will entail a good deal of disagreement. Arguments will occur. Tempers will flare. Thus, it is important that emotions be expressed openly and honestly and that opponents come together to work out their differences. If this occurs, conflict may become a source of strength rather than a sign of weakness.

Surprisingly, the key to changing the church's attitude toward conflict lies with the pastors more than the laymen. Of course, as our study indicates, many laymen desire the church to be a place of peace and "reconciliation." Nevertheless, the laymen, with their experience in the hard realities of the commercial world, are often quite used to conflict. Pastors, on the other hand, are frequently afraid of conflict. They feel guilt when conflict disrupts the peace that they have been taught to value in their congregations. Furthermore, they are at a loss as to how conflict should be handled. Thus, it is often the pastor who tries to suppress tensions within his parish.

Theological seminaries are at least partially to blame for having failed to prepare their students to handle conflict creatively. Seminary education, in practical theology, has had two main emphases, preaching and counseling. These tools although necessary, are not sufficient to prepare a pastor for life in the multi-church where conflict has become a reality of parish life. Today's pastor must have two additional qualifications: technical competence in the art of conflict management and personal ability to engage in conflict without undue anxiety. Thus, we suggest that at least two additional courses become highly recommended items in the seminary curriculum. First, the social ethics department should have a full course in the dynamics of conflict and the techniques of conflict management. Second, the psychology department should offer courses based on the principle of the encounter group. Students should have experience in honest emotional confrontation with others so that they learn not to fear such situations.

If, in addition, students can be induced to engage in some real community conflicts, the experience gained could be invaluable.

In order to be successful the attitudinal changes suggested above must be accompanied by important structural changes. Most of these changes will be at the level of the parish, but before turning to these we shall mention several possible reforms at higher levels of the church structure. One important change concerns the purpose and content of presbytery meetings. These meetings have traditionally been concerned with detailed administrative matters and have allowed very little time for open discussion of controversial issues. If, as we predict, the regional committees and staff leaders increasingly take over the job of generating prophetic action programs, then it becomes critical that presbyterys and synods have a forum for expression and debate. In short, the presbytery docket should be liberated from administrative details and set free for encounter on substantive matters.

There is also an urgent need for a specialized presbytery committee whose purpose is to promote the confrontation of adversaries and the honest expression of differences. Thus, for example, there should have been a committee with responsibility to bring the opposition leaders on the Alinsky matter together for the airing of grievances. Perhaps if the two sides had unloaded all their anger in an encounter group, they might have come to a far better understanding and adjustment. The open hatred that existed among presbytery leaders and the lack of channels for expression of this hatred certainly promoted the destructive aspects of the controversy.

Another possible reform concerns the use of clergy teams. In our congregation studies, we were impressed with the advantages of the multiple staff in coping with difficult issues. At Westminster, for example, the five-man staff was able to develop tactics based on a division of labor. While Dr. Hope took a moderate position, Mr. Barton was able to appeal to the conservatives, and Mr. Pressman was assigned responsibilities for developing alternative action programs. In short, West-minster, the classic multi-church, was able to mobilize different men to deal with the different factions. Obviously, however, not all churches can afford to hire five pastors. Thus, for the smaller churches, clergy teams might be useful. The team members could specialize in different aspects of the ministry. If a parishioner came in with questions about urban problems, he could be referred to the urban expert. The suggestion of team ministries is based on the judgment that the single "general practitioner" pastor will be swamped by the multiple interests of the multi-church.

Structural changes are also needed at the local parish level. These changes may be summarized as specialization, co-optation, and institutionalization of conflict. A preliminary matter, however, concerns the "recognition" that the church has become a multi-church. Many churchmen, both clergy and laity alike, have been clinging to the passwords of bygone days. For them, the church is, above all, "one holy and indivisible body." They have studiously refused to see the growing division within church ranks concerning purposes and goals. The facts must be faced. The church does have a split personality. Local parishes can work creatively only if the leaders have a clear reading of parishioner attitudes. For these reasons, we suggest that an annual "survey of attitudes" be taken of all members. A brief questionnaire should be used to gain information concerning overall congregational positions on major issues and individual likes and dislikes. Delineating these concerns is essential for any pastor who subscribes to Dietrich Bonhoeffer's conception of the church, namely, a place where human existence is understood and clarified.

The first suggestion for structural reform of the local parish is specialization. This represents a continuation of a trend that has already begun. As the church branches out into multiple avenues representing its multiple interests, it can no longer rely on a handful of general leaders. The laity must be mobilized to carry out their self-understanding of their Christian vocation and ministry. "Task forces" is a term that has recently been adopted in some parishes for the kind of program envisaged. The task force is an action committee composed of members with special interest in particular problem areas. Appointment to these working groups may be based on the information received from the annual questionnaires. The specialized action committee, then, should be encouraged to move boldly in its area of concern, more boldly than the congregation as a whole would be expected to move. In short, since consensus politics in the multi-church is tantamount to inaction, the action committee or task force becomes an alternative to total immobilization.

If specialization represents the alternative to inaction, then "co-optation" represents the alternative to polarization and destructive internal warfare. The basic principle of co-optation is that every action committee should include representatives of that portion of the congregation which opposes the specified form of action. This ensures that the opposition position will receive clear expression during the actual process of deliberation and decision-making. Co-optation has a double function. First, it ensures that the various wings of the congregation will exercise a critical and challenging influence on each other. Conservatives may challenge liberals to be authentically and effectively liberal, and liberals may similarly demand genuine action rather than evasion from their conservative brethren. Second, co-optation functions to keep controversy in the open so that it will not go under the surface into clandestine interest groups.

In conjunction with co-optation, the specialized action groups should to some degree have interlocking memberships. The primary purpose of this tactic is to prevent the groups from polarizing down a ready-made line of cleavage. We have previously commented on the disastrous effects of the structural split between the liberals and conservatives at Fargo. Unless the various groups are tied together structurally, they will tend to become secretive and hostile combat groups in times of strain, and bases for communication will be tenuous.

In short, the local parish must walk the line between the Scylla of inaction and the Charybdis of civil war. This can best be done through the combination which we have suggested: clear recognition of differences, specialization of effort, co-optation of opposition viewpoints, and interlocking memberships. These suggestions, however, do not include the promise of freedom from conflict. Far from it. As we have argued in the previous chapter, conflict is unavoidable in the multichurch. Thus, in addition to co-optation and structural interlinkages in the action committees, structural reform must be undertaken for the special purpose of conflict management.

The single most pressing need uncovered by our study is that each parish have a permanent institution whose sole purpose is to provide a forum for the airing of conflict. This committee should not be charged with responsibility for substantive decision or action. Its function should be to provide a place where adversaries can face each other and give expression to the emotional hostilities and blockages that have developed. Without unnecessary snooping or prying, the conflict committee should encourage the airing of suppressed tension and grievances.

The conflict committe should have access to trained encounter group leaders. In its own operation, it should promote the kind of honest confrontation that is the goal of encounter groups. The committee should also encourage the formation of permanent encounter groups within the congregation, and it should be able to develop short-term *ad hoc* encounter groups for dealing with more specific tensions. Perhaps an optimal arrangement would be to have encounter groups which crosscut the action groups in membership and provide a secondary means of interlocking membership. It is interesting to note that a number of the new religious movements in postwar Japan have institutionalized encounter groups that are referred to as "HOZA." The HOZA is a small, face-to-face group that meets regularly to share burdens, sorrows, and grievances, and thus minister to one another (See Robert Lee, *Stranger in the Land,* pp. 142 ff.; Friendship Press, 1967.)

We feel strongly that the conflict committee is a critical necessity for life in the multi-church. Astonishingly, not one of our congregation had anything like such a committee. In fact, the only congregation that had any permanent forum for airing conflict was Park Street, whose "concerns of the church" period during worship service functioned in this way. The absence of such a forum was felt most strongly at Westminster, where despite much exposure to conflict situations the members felt the absence of any approved means for confrontation and expression of differences. For this reason, Dr. Hope, of Westminster, recommends that session meetings be open to all members as they were at Christ Church during the Alinsky debate. Surely this would be a step in the right direction. Nevertheless, we feel that a separate conflict committee would be far better.

Church leaders should continue to search out and identify mechanisms for creative conflict management.

The few guidelines suggested in the last two chapters for life in the multi-church of course do not exhaust either the needs or the possibilities of today's church. Nevertheless, it is our hope that this case study of conflict over community organization has served to focus attention on a critical problem area and that the proposed reforms will at least point in the direction of renewal and vitality for the church, which faces a future destined to be filled with conflict.